Europe by Train

Backpacking for Beginners

Julian Trometer

ISBN: 9798695597981

© Copyright 2020 Julian Trometer - All contents, especially texts, photographs, and graphics, are protected by copyright. All rights, including reproduction, publication, editing, and translation, are reserved.

Foreword

You want to discover the world, but you don't like sitting in an airplane for hours, or you don't like being stuck in traffic jams? Then this book is just the right one for you. It is written for all those who want to travel in a relaxed way, namely by train.

A common reason why many people hesitate to travel is the fear of the unknown. This is a great pity because countless adventures and exciting experiences await you once you have taken the first step.

This is why this book contains a great deal of information about train travel, Europe, and the Interrail Pass. The book will help you make the right decisions when planning your journey and plan your route in detail. Your questions are answered and supplemented with the experiences of other travelers.

I do not want to tell you what to do, but rather show you what is possible. The vision behind it is to inspire you, give you courage, and give you an unforgettable experience.

Julian Trometer

Table of Contents

1. Introduction 8
   About the Author 8
   Why Travel by Train? 10
   The Adventure Awaits! 10
   Experience With Train Travel 12

2. Travel Possibilities 24
   Single Train Tickets 24
   Eurail Pass 25
   Interrail Pass 25
   Other Travel Options 29
   Booking Portals 29

3. Travel Partner 30
   Rather Travel Alone? 30
   Get to Know People 32
   Travel With Travel Partners? 34
   Find Travel Partners 36

4. Route Planning 38
   Planning Methods 38
   Seat Reservations 41
   Popular Interrail Routes 46

Popular Night Train Routes *55*
Countries & Highlights................................*58*
   Central Europe 58
   Scandinavia 63
   Southern Europe 66
   Eastern Europe...................................68
   Balkan Region.....................................71

5. Accommodation **77**
Hostels..*78*
Holiday Flats..*80*
Couchsurfing..*81*
BeWelcome *82*
HelpX *83*
Hotels *83*
Camping *84*

6. Budget Planning...................................**85**
Costs for Train Tickets *85*
Reservation Costs *87*
Expenditure per Destination....................*90*
Cut Expenses...*91*
Pay On the Way......................................*94*
Keep the Overview..................................*95*

7. Equipment 96
Backpack *97*
Clothing *99*
Toilet Bag *101*
Documents *102*
Camping *103*
Miscellaneous..*103*
Travel Guide *104*
Unnecessary *107*
How Much to Pack?..*108*

8. Safety 109
Securing Documents..*109*
Pickpocketing *110*
Identity Card Lost *110*
Credit Card Lost *111*
Smartphone Lost *113*
Security for Women...*114*
Outdoor Safety *116*

9. Health 117
Emergency Telephone Numbers..............................*117*
European Health Card *118*
International Health Insurance *120*

Vaccinations & Precaution *121*

10. Practical Tips **123**
Tips for Train Travel..*126*

Tips for Thrifty *130*

Cooking Tips *135*

Tips for Adventurers *140*

Travel Diary & Blog...*141*

11. Conclusion **142**

1. Introduction

About the Author

During the first semester break of my studies, I decided to try an Interrail tour. At that time, I went to the station with a little skepticism: Is a trip through Europe worthwhile at all? I have often traveled by train throughout Germany, so what else should I expect? The biggest adventure of my life awaited me, although I had seen so much of the world already.

The photo was taken during a trip through Romania.

When I was 21, I decided to spend a year working & traveling in Australia. This was my first experience alone in the big world and far away from home. For me, at that time, a great experience and something I would not want to miss. During this trip, I soon realized that Australia is not as spectacular as everyone has always claimed. Sure, to see a koala up close or to meet kangaroos at the campsite is insanely beautiful, but only because it is new and unknown. For example, Australians love Europe because, for them, it is the distant, unexplored continent. During this trip, countless travelers worldwide have told me how beautiful Europe is and how lucky I am to have such cultural diversity in such a small area.

At some point, it became clear to me that I only made the trip to Australia because many people had been there before me and reported about it. But I hadn't seen much of Europe and didn't know most of the destinations, as they are not written about very often. That's why I only had Australia in my mind the whole time and not a single alternative. For an adventure, no far-off destination is necessary because adventures are waiting everywhere!

Since I realized this, I regularly travel by train and explore cities, hike in nature, or do other activities. I have met so many different people during these adventures, and I could get to know Europe's diversity. I have decided to publish a book. I would like to inspire you with it, give you courage, and give you an unforgettable experience.

Why Travel by Train?

Europe has an excellent rail network and trains leave every hour in all directions. With the right ticket, you can use almost all trains and travel through Europe with great flexibility. Traveling by train is the best way to explore Europe and experience adventure. While others travel to distant countries and pay a lot of money for the flight to find the ultimate travel experience, they often miss the breathtaking beauty of Europe right on their own doorstep.

- You will meet travelers from all over the world.
- You discover new and exciting places in Europe.
- You save money because Europe is affordable.
- You experience unforgettable adventures.
- You travel more sustainably and protect your environment.

The Adventure Awaits!

I felt great uncertainty in me before I went on my first long journey. On the one hand, I was traveling alone. On the other hand, I was going to Australia, several thousand kilometers away from home. The uncertainty was so overwhelming that I thought several times that I might not go on the trip after all. Fortunately, I decided against my feeling. Right on the first day, I met other backpackers who felt the same way I did. They all went through the same thing and luckily decided to travel. After the first week of traveling alone, the many new friends and different circumstances had become routine for me.

Today I look back on the many small and big experiences and how I have grown through them. My horizon has broadened enormously. Now I can make a trip at any time without much planning and feel no fear or uncertainty. I also have much more confidence in myself and do not think about possible problems months in advance. Instead, I take off straight away and use all the opportunities offered to me on my travels. You can do the same. You just have to dare! Already Pericles, one of the leading statesmen of Athens, said in the 5th century B.C.: *"The secret to happiness is freedom, and the secret to freedom is courage."*

Experience With Train Travel

Interrail has been in existence since 1972, and several hundred thousand people use the pass every year. The experiences are consistently positive, and many travelers report exciting experiences throughout Europe. For this reason, I have asked interrailers about their experiences and have compiled the answers here. In addition to these experiences, I also present the respective route, including tips for the train routes.

"To get on a train and know that a city undiscovered is waiting for you is an overwhelming feeling."
Paul

"Interrail makes your dream of adventure come true!"
Lisa

"You meet people from all over the world and learn to appreciate the travel opportunities in Europe."
Leonie

"Our tour of Europe was just brilliant!"
Nina

"Traveling with Interrail means not only discovering Europe but also getting to know yourself from a different side."
Tom

"Even if you travel alone, you are never alone."
Amelie

"Traveling through Europe is simply the the best mix of culture and adventure."
Lena

"Interrail is worthwhile for all those who, after graduation or studies, need time off."
Thilo

"We have visited countless museums and explored many new cities."
Frank & Laura

Amelie's Field Report - Traveling Alone

I did an Interrail tour last year in May, shortly after my 18th birthday. I started alone, but during the trip, I was always with other backpackers. This was a new experience for me, but traveling alone is absolutely no problem. In hostels, you get to know people very quickly for everyday activities and travel routes.

Itinerary: Prague > Vienna > Salzburg > Venice > Rome > Florence > Milan > Paris > Bruges > Geneva > Amsterdam

Accommodations: During the trip, I mostly accommodated in hostels and slept two nights on the night train. Once from Salzburg to Venice and once from Milan to Paris. I could always sleep very well on night trains. In the hostels, it was a bit louder, depending on the number of beds.

Budget: Hostels & food 1.093€ + Interrail-pass with discount 333€ + reservation costs 93€ = 1.519€

Highlights: During my trip, I particularly enjoyed the fairytale city of Bruges. Furthermore, I liked Paris, Amsterdam, and Florence very much. However, I was not in these cities in the high season.

I'd do Better Next Time: A day trip to Brussels was very dull and nothing compared to Bruges. I wouldn't revisit Milan either, as it is too touristy there.

Tip: Use night trains; you save a night in a hostel and are already at another place the next day. The routes from Salzburg to Venice and from Milan to Paris are highly recommended.

Conclusion: My trip through Europe was an absolute dream, and I would do it again anytime. My experiences as a single traveler are excellent. You don't have to worry, because you get to know other travelers super fast. You start alone, but then you always have other travelers around you.

Waiting for the train to Salzburg.

Thilo's Field Report - Cities & Parties

My name is Thilo (25), and I was traveling with two other Swiss guys (23 & 26) for a month with the Interrail ticket. We were able to gain a lot of new experiences and got to know some cities. We traveled aimlessly from day to day and from town to town. We always looked for accommodation and trains spontaneously. Since we like to go out in the evening, we picked out the party cities in Europe. There are excellent parties not only in the clubs but also in the one or the other hostel.

Itinerary: Vienna > Paris > Barcelona > Berlin > Stockholm > Amsterdam > Vienna

Accommodations: Couchsurfing, Airbnb & Hostels

Budget: Accommodation, food & activities: 1.322€, Interrail-pass 301€ & reservations 150€.

Highlights: We almost always stay with couchsurfers, which is a very exciting and varied experience. The acceptances often come spontaneously, but you get to know people from other cities who can give you some insider tips. We were able to get to know the most different quarters through the different hosts. Finding a host who can accommodate three travelers at once is not exactly easy, but it is possible. The good thing about couchsurfing is that you save a lot of money and get to know people from the city who travel themselves.

I'd Do Better Next Time: I would book reservations in advance because many journeys on my route required reservations. Mostly we booked spontaneously and therefore spent almost 150€. If you don't have a reservation, you either have to pay an expensive extra charge, or the conductor will drop you off at the next station. A conductor in Vienna caught us, but luckily he made an exception.

Tip: Travel shorter distances by train, because you get more out of it. We often took the train up to 15h and once even almost 26h from Barcelona to Berlin. This is very exhausting, and you quickly reach your limits.

Conclusion: We enjoyed it very much. We got to know many couchsurfers and experienced some excellent parties. Interrail is worthwhile for all those who need some time off after graduation or studies.

Rubens Field Report - Interrail

I come from the Netherlands, and I have already traveled through Europe twice with Interrail. The good thing about Interrail is that you can travel to any city without a lot of preparation and move on when you have had enough. Sometimes it is difficult to find the right train, but that makes the adventure unique—the first trip we did as a couple, and the second one I did alone. Traveling alone is much more fun, but traveling in pairs is more relaxed because you always have someone on the train.

Itinerary: Amsterdam > Prague > Budapest > Košice > Vienna > Wörgl > Milan

Kolín > Košice > Bratislava (via Telgárt) > Holland > Hamburg > Innsbruck > Zurich > Copenhagen > Malmö > Berlin > Holland

Accommodations: Mostly hostels and a few times, I used couchsurfing. Both perfect to meet travelers.

Highlights: Take the night train! You fall asleep in one city and wake up in the next. The best night train experience I had was from Malmö to Berlin. You can watch the sunset on the high seas in the evening and be in Berlin for breakfast.

Other highlights of my trip were the small Happy Bull

Hostel in Košice and Slovakia, and the Czech Republic. Both countries are lovely and also very cheap to travel to.

Tip: Bring playing cards for the train rides, bring presents for your couchsurfing hosts, and "Go with the Flow!"

Conclusion: For the last two years, I have been traveling with Interrail, and this year I will start my third journey. I can say that traveling alone is fun from my experiences, but it is more pleasant when traveling in pairs.

Nina's Experience Report – Interrail in a Group

Two years ago, we journeyed with the Interrail ticket through Belgium, France, Italy, and Portugal. We were on the road as a group of three girls, and in the three and a half weeks, we discovered that Interrail is merely ingenious. We used the 10-days-pass, and for the return trip, we took a flight because we recently lacked travel time. We enjoyed the trip very much and were able to gain great experiences.

Itinerary: Liège > Luxembourg > Paris > Venice > Florence > Barcelona > Madrid > Lisbon > Lagos > Porto

Highlights: We liked Venice, Madrid, and Lisbon best. Portugal is a beautiful, inexpensive country and wildly popular with surfers.

Accommodations: Since there were three of us, Airbnb was the cheapest place for us to stay. But we spent five nights in an eight-bedroom in a hostel and two on night trains.

Budget: Altogether we spent, apart from the reservation and equipment costs, 1260€ for the trip.

I'd Do Better Next Time: The first ride with the night train from Paris to Venice was a disaster, and we couldn't sleep. The second trip from Madrid to Lisbon, on the other hand, was a dream and very relaxed.

Tip: In any case, take a few euros more with you. We did not plan enough cash, as we saw the false information in travel forums. Especially in the more known cities as Paris or Nizza, the accommodations and food are costly.

Conclusion: Our Interrail tour was simply brilliant! But next time we will take more time and money with us because then we can go back by train and don't have to look at the prices all the time.

Lena's Experience Report - Woman, Traveling Alone

I traveled alone by train through France and the surrounding area, and I have to say that this is the easiest way to travel and the most beautiful. The experiences I had with the other travelers during this time were consistently positive, and I was able to gain many new impressions.

Itinerary: Amsterdam > Paris > Barcelona > Marseille > Toulon > Genova > Bologna > Innsbruck

Accommodation: Only hostels and one night in a hotel

Highlights: The cultures change with every train ride. Europe is so diverse, which I would not have expected. One day I visited the Louvre in Paris, and the next day I took a walk on the beach in Barcelona. On the one hand, you can enjoy city life, and on the other hand, you can be out in nature. This is a lot of fun, and I immediately felt like having another travel adventure.

I'd Do Better Next Time: On my next trip, I'll be carrying less luggage. First, I pack all things; later, I unpack all items again and then pack everything another time. In the long run, it quickly gets annoying if you have taken too much with you.

Tip: Write down all the contact information, such as your accommodation address and telephone number. This will give you a good overview of the accommodation you have booked, and you will know which ones you still have to book. This travel plan will also help you if your mobile phone is empty or if you don't have an internet connection.

Conclusion: The train tour was a lovely experience that I often think back to. It is simply the best mixture of city and country as well as culture and adventure. If you have the opportunity, then definitely take a trip by train.

2. Travel Possibilities

There are precisely two options for train tickets. One is to buy individual tickets, and the other is to use an Interrail pass. Both have advantages and disadvantages, depending on how long you want to travel and how flexible you want to be.

Single Train Tickets

Buying individual tickets is suitable for a long weekend or a whole week in another city. It is also a good option for a short trip. You should buy these a few months in advance because that's when they are cheapest. If you only want to travel to one or two places and have a fixed travel date, this is the best option for you. However, separate tickets are not suitable for flexible travel, as they are costly for short-term purchases.

I have already explored many cities. For example, I have traveled from Berlin to Gdansk or from Bielefeld to Antwerp. I booked these trips for three to six months in advance because I wanted to experience something on the planned weekends.

Eurail Pass

Confusion about Interrail and Eurail occurs repeatedly, so here is a brief explanation of the tickets. The tickets are similar, but it depends on where you come from. If you are a European citizen, you can use the Interrail pass. If you are not a European citizen, you can travel with the Eurail pass. If you live permanently in Europe but are not a European citizen, you can still travel with the Interrail pass. All you have to show is a certificate of residence in Europe. All the information valid for the Interrail Pass is also right for the Eurail Pass.

Interrail Pass

An Interrail pass, also known as an Interrail ticket, is suitable for longer journeys and spontaneous travel planning. You do not have to plan in advance but can decide where you want to go when you get to the track. The pass is worthwhile for journeys from one week up to three months. So if you're going to travel longer and don't want to commit yourself, an Interrail Pass is the best option for you. The passports are available in a variety of designs. They differ according to the duration, the countries, and whether you have individual travel days or travel in one piece.

I traveled for several weeks through the Netherlands, Belgium, and France with the Interrail Pass and did the travel planning very spontaneously. The only thing that was fixed was a rough route, which changed several times during the trip. It was a maximum travel time of six weeks because then the university started again.

Basically, the Interrail Pass has various options that differ in travel duration, countries, and flexibility.

One Country & Global Pass

The One Country Pass allows you to travel through exactly one country and is therefore slightly cheaper. The states are divided into categories and differ slightly in cost. The Global Pass allows you to travel through all 32 participating Interrail countries. The great advantage is that you don't have to commit yourself and are more flexible. You can spontaneously make a side trip to another state or change your travel plans entirely on-site. Most Interrailer use this passport because of its flexibility. You have to decide for yourself which Interrail passport is suitable for you.

Once you have chosen the right passport, the decision of the travel days comes up to you. You have to decide the length of your journey and how many days you want to travel. Either you buy a Flexi Pass, which allows you to travel a certain number of days, use it for up to two months, or book a Continuous Pass. You can travel between 15 days and three months at a time.

Flexible & Continuous-Pass

A Flexi Pass allows you to use up a certain number of days of travel within a month or two. You can choose the days you want to travel and use them spontaneously. Most interrailers use the Flexi-Pass to travel more relaxed and save money.

With a Continuous Pass, you can travel every day of the booked period. The Continuous Pass is slightly more expensive than the Flexi Pass. Still, you can travel every day, and you are not limited in the number of days you can travel. Interrailers who are traveling for two or three months use this pass usually.

4 - 5 Days Flexi Pass - Enough for a one or two week trip to explore a country or a small country trip, such as Poland, to the Czech Republic.

7 - 10 Days Flexi Pass - Suitable for up to one month of Interrail and the exploration of several contiguous countries, such as the Benelux countries.

15-Day Flexi Pass - Ideal for a long train journey and for exploring more distant countries such as Greece or Portugal.

15 - 22 Days Continuous Pass - Do you want to see a different city every other day and explore as many metropolises as possible in two to three weeks? Then this is your pass.

1 - 3 Months Continuous Pass - You want to explore Europe's whole and travel from north to west and south to east? Then one of the monthly passes is best suited for you.

Which train ticket fits you best?

Other Travel Options

Another way to travel in Europe is by bus or by car. This sounds a bit out of place in a book about train travel. But in some countries, it makes sense because of the lack of rail connections. For example, suppose you are traveling to Albania, where you cannot use the Interrail Pass or need more days of travel than your Interrail Pass allows. In that case, a trip by bus can help. In most cases, traveling by train is possible and also the best way to travel. You can find suitable bus tickets on the following search portals.

Booking Portals

Interrail & Eurail ⇒ Interrail.eu & Eurail.com

Rail

- ⇒ raileurope.com
- ⇒ thetrainline.com
- ⇒ omio.com
- ⇒ rome2rio.com
- ⇒ fromatob.com
- ⇒ virail.com

Bus

- ⇒ omio.com
- ⇒ blablacar.com
- ⇒ rome2rio.com
- ⇒ fromatob.com
- ⇒ virail.com
- ⇒ busbud.com

3. Travel Partner

Search queries on travel partner portals are multiplying, as there are more and more travelers who would rather travel in pairs than alone. What most people forget, however, is that a trip alone can also be a fantastic experience if you get involved. Therefore, here you can find out about the advantages and disadvantages of traveling alone or in pairs.

Rather Travel Alone?

You would like to experience an Interrail adventure but don't have anyone who wants to come along? Or do you want to travel alone and are unsure if that is a good idea? Traveling alone in Europe is no problem, even as a woman traveling alone because all European countries are safe. Especially for travel beginners, it is an excellent opportunity to try out traveling alone. Your personality will grow through new experiences, and you will also meet many new people. I started most of my trips alone and then met other travelers in hostels or during activities. Actually, with a few small exceptions, there was always someone around me. So new friendships were quickly made, and I had lots of excellent conversations about all kinds of topics. For example, I traveled with a millionaire from Liechtenstein, a Swedish diving instructor, or an Italian architect who lives in Paris' heart. This would not have happened to me if I had been traveling with a travel partner. So don't let yourself be deterred from your plans even without a travel partner. Just start alone, meet new people, and come back with new friends.

Advantages of Traveling Alone

- You will get to know travelers who have plans similar to yours, and you will not have to convince anyone to come with you on an Interrail journey. You might even meet someone with different travel plans, join them, and discover other exciting places than you had planned.
- You get to know new people and travel more individually, as you may even have several travel partners. This will increase your self-confidence because you are prepared for changing people and different adventures.
- If you have other travel plans, find a new travel partner. Disagreements and discussions can occur with a fixed travel partner. On my first trip, I met two backpackers who fell out with each other so severely that they were no longer friends after the trip.

Get to Know People

- Greet other people and learn to understand their reactions. For example, if you sit down in your seat on a train, greet your neighbor directly, and see if he or she reacts positively. Perhaps a conversation will develop out of it. I have started perfect conversations through this method and was recently invited by my seat neighbor for a beer in the Boardbistro.
- Stay mainly in hostels, as you can quickly make contacts in the common room and while cooking. Hostels are also relatively cheap, and you will sleep in a multi-bedroom where you will meet other travelers. Just say hello to your roommates. Most people are quite shy and don't dare to talk to other travelers. Therefore, I always introduce myself directly, my name, and where my next destination is. For example, shortly after I arrived in Paris, I cooked with my room neighbor and exchanged travel tips. In the evening, we explored the city by night.
- As an alternative to hostels, simply use couchsurfing and get to know hosts from the respective travel country. The advantage is that you get local insider tips and accommodation directly. Still, you don't meet a travel partner for the rest of your journey. However, I do not

recommend couchsurfing for young women traveling alone—more about this in the accommodation chapter.
- Use the Couchsurfing Hangout function to get to know other travelers in your area. The app shows you other couchsurfers and what they want to experience in the respective city. Some want to meet for lunch, visit a museum or go to a party and you can join them. Hangouts are also very suitable for women traveling alone, as you don't have to stay overnight with them and therefore don't have to rely on them. I have met other travelers in several cities and was invited to Austria by a female couchsurfer, among others.
- Visit local events and meet locals or other travelers. On Couchsurfing, MeetUp, or Facebook, there are always events suggested to you depending on the location. On Facebook, it's mostly everyday events with people at the respective site; on Couchsurfing, it's usually more travelers than locals, and on MeetUp, it's a balanced mix depending on the city.
- In Facebook groups, interrailers regularly write about the city they are currently in and whether someone wants to meet them. This is one of the best ways to get to know other

interrailers or get tips for the respective city. You can find possible Facebook groups here:
- Interrail Travelers Official
- Interrail Travelers
- #DiscoverEU Official

Travel With Travel Partners?

Traveling with a travel partner or in a group can be a great experience. You can gather experiences together, rely on each other, and look back on shared memories years later. The good thing is that you never have to travel alone and always have someone to talk to. You will meet fewer people on your journey, but you will have other advantages.

Advantages of a Travel Partner

- You already know your travel partner, and you have the same travel plans. After the journey, there will be a pleasant, shared memory. You may have good experiences with changing travel partners, but you can't share them easily with the respective persons.
- You have a greater sense of security because you know and trust each other. Europe is a safe place to travel, but the feeling of being able to rely on someone is even better for the perceived safety.
- You don't have to take or pay for everything twice because you don't have everything in your luggage twice or share the costs. For example, if you take a travel hairdryer, you only need one. You can also save on accommodation costs by booking a double room. This is more expensive than staying in a multi-bedroom, but sometimes you might want to have a little more privacy.

Find Travel Partners

There are two ways to find a travel partner. One is to find someone before the trip, and the other is to meet someone during the trip. Both have their advantages and disadvantages, and you should consider which is the better option for you before traveling. Here are some recommendations:

- Tell your friends in the time that you want to go on a journey. Maybe someone from your circle of friends already has the same idea or decides to come along because they do not want to travel alone. If your friends know that you are going on a journey and are still looking for a travel partner, they can ask their friends and acquaintances. This increases your search radius enormously. If someone wants to come along, you already know the person through someone else.
- There are several Interrail groups on Facebook in which requests are regularly posted, and suitable travel partners are found. You can either actively search for posts from other Interrailers looking for a fellow traveler or create one yourself. You will soon find someone with the same route, travel time, and interests. You will also spontaneously find

travel partners for a few days in a city or for single route sections in the groups.
- o Interrail Travelers Official
- o Interrail Travelers
- o #DiscoverEU Official

Tip: In addition to the recommended groups, other groups are only valid for the current or coming year. Just search for "Interrail + Year" on Facebook.

Tip: Post a picture of yourself and an approximate route, so the chances increase enormously.

- On travel partner search engines, you can find possible travel partners at the push of a button. All you have to do is search for the keyword "Interrail," and other backpackers will be suggested. If you can't find one that suits you, you can also submit a free search yourself.

Tip: If you publish a post yourself, upload meaningful pictures of yourself with a short description. The description should show your itinerary or possible destinations as well as your travel time. If you don't have any exact plans yet and are open to everything, you can, of course, mention that.

4. Route Planning

Finding a suitable Interrail route is not so easy. On the one hand, you want to see as many cities as possible, and on the other hand, you don't want to sit on the train for an extended period. You will find all the vital information about the countries and routes here. So you can make it easier for you to plan your route and give you the best possible Interrail experience.

Planning Methods

Once you have decided on a travel period, you can start planning your route directly. A handy tool is the Interrail map, which you will receive as a printed version when you buy your ticket. It contains all roads, including the duration of the journey and ferry connections, and express train routes. Before planning your trip, please note the costs of the respective country. My cost calculation will give you a good overview. Once the travel countries have been determined, you can start planning your route. There are three methods for planning your trip to find the ideal way.

List Method - With the List Method, you create a list of countries and cities you want to see. You then prioritize these and plan your route. The advantage of this method is that you can visit your preferred cities and countries individually. The disadvantage is that you have to do the complete route planning and cancel some cities or countries due to time constraints.

Return Trip Method - With the Return Trip Method, you only plan the return trip from a city of your choice. Your goal is to reach that city at the time of the train's departure. This method's advantage is that your return journey is already secured, and you will be home on time. This method's disadvantage is that you are bound to your destination and cannot spontaneously drive in a completely different direction.

Modification Method - With the Modification Method, you use pre-planned routes and modify them according to your wishes. You can find the routes a few pages further on in this chapter or in the experience reports of Interrailers. The advantage of this method is that the routes have already been traveled. You only have to worry about the exact departure times of the trains. If you don't like a city, you can delete it from the route and look for an alternative. This method saves you a lot of time when planning and uses the inspiration of other travelers.

> **Tip:** Detailed planning of the Interrail route is a lot of fun and offers you a certain security amount. But you should always leave yourself the option of changing your course spontaneously and let yourself drift. True to the motto: *"Life is what happens while you're making other Interrail plans."*

Europe offers you a whole lot of countries you can travel to. It's not easy to keep track and make a decision. Here is a brief assessment of the regions in terms of costs, comfort, and experience.

	Budget	**Comfort**	**Experience**
Scandinavia	€€€€	high	none
Central Europe	€€€€	high	none
Southern Europe	€€€	high	none
Eastern Europe	€€	low	some
Balkans	€	low	some

Seat Reservations

Depending on which countries your Interrail tour passes through and how fast you want to travel, you may or may not need reservations. You should bear this in mind when planning your route, as it will incur extra costs. If you are on a tight budget, you can either travel through countries without reservations or use slower trains, thus avoiding seat reservations. If you have a more extensive account, you can secure a seat on one of the high-speed or night trains. I will explain in more detail later which countries these are and what costs you will have to pay. Right now, the first question is whether a seat reservation is always necessary.

Mostly Requiring a Reservation - For these countries, you must make a reservation for almost all trains. Without a reservation, you cannot use the trains requiring a reservation, as you will be fined on the train. You can determine whether a reservation is necessary for the Interrail App or by looking at the small R behind the train connections.

- France
- Greece
- Italy
- Spain

Partially Reservation Required - Reservations are not always needed in these countries, but they may be depending on the train. Here, too, the Interrail app will help you find out which trains require a reservation.

- Bosnia & Herzegovina
- Bulgaria
- Croatia
- Czech Republic
- Denmark
- Finland
- Hungary
- Norway
- Poland
- Portugal
- Romania
- Serbia
- Slovenia
- Sweden
- Switzerland

No Reservation Necessary - In these countries, no reservation is necessary, and you can simply start without much planning. However, depending on the season and the day, a reservation can make sense.

- Austria
- Belgium
- Germany
- Ireland
- Luxembourg
- Montenegro
- Netherlands
- Slovakia
- Turkey

Tip: Even if a reservation is not necessary, it can be quite useful. Especially during rush hours or holiday periods, it can be swamped. However, capacity utilization also depends strongly on the connection and time of day. For example, if you are traveling in the low season and a reservation is optional, you can save yourself money. However, if you travel long distances and during the holiday season, you can play it safe by making a reservation.

Tip: Fare evasion is not recommended. If you use a train requiring a reservation without a reservation and get caught, you will be fined and have to get off. There are always friendly inspectors who will turn a blind eye or just let you get off, but this is not the rule.

Book Reservations

Once you have planned your approximate Interrail route and know the trains that require reservations, you should book your seat reservations. Depending on the train company, the costs will increase, and there is a limited contingent for some routes. Therefore, it makes sense to book as soon as possible. If you realize afterward that you no longer need the reservation, you can simply return it. To do so, go to the ticket counter at the station and return the reservation before you start your journey. The amount will be refunded, and you will not have made a loss.

There are two ways to make a seat reservation. You either book the reservation directly at the station at the ticket counter or book the reservation online. Depending on the country, you can also book the reservation online and print it out at the nearest station. Booking a reservation on the train is usually not possible and may be subject to a penalty. Therefore, it is better to look for a suitable connection in advance and make a reservation.

Book Online - To book your reservation online, you need to go to Interrail.eu and log in with your account. If you don't have an account yet, you can easily create one. All you need is your personal details, your Interrail pass number, and a credit card or other payment method. You then log in with your account, choose your preferred route and book one or more reservations. You can also reserve seats for your travel partners so that you can sit next to each other.

Attention: There is not an electronic reservation for all trains. Some reservations must be sent to you by mail, which can take up to a week. This means that you either have to reserve in time or print out the reservation at the nearest machine as it is possible in France.

Offline Booking - Another way to book a reservation for Interrail is to do this at the station. You choose your desired connection in advance, and the staff at the information desk will book it for you. You must remember to mention your Interrail pass, as Interrail reservations may differ from standard reservations.

Popular Interrail Routes

Eastern Europe for Beginners

Prague > Krakow > Warsaw

7 Days thereof 5 Travel Days

Eastern Europe is big and to see everything necessary you should take at least a month. If you don't have that much time, five days of travel are already enough to get a small insight into the Eastern European culture. Starting in the Czech Republic capital, Prague, the journey takes you through student Krakow to the Polish capital Warsaw. Besides affordable beer and good food, there is a distinct backpacker culture here. There are a lot of hostels that offer tours through the nightlife. If you like it a bit quieter and prefer to spend a day relaxing on the beach, you can go on an excursion to Gdansk from Warsaw. The Gdansk beach is only a few minutes away from the city center.

Tip: In Eastern Europe, trains are occasionally delayed for more extended periods, so you should definitely pack a good book or audiobook.

Italy's Pizza Express

Zurich > Milan > Florence > Rome > Naples > Sicily > Livorno > Pisa > Venice > Innsbruck

30 Days thereof 10 Travel Days

Italy is known worldwide not only for its excellent ice cream but also for its exquisite pizza. This route takes you through all the famous Italian cities in just ten days and gives you tips on the best pizzerias. The route starts in the fashion metropolis of Milan, takes you to Naples, the birthplace of pizza, and ends in Venice. This itinerary has been created in search of the best pizza and, therefore, leads through Italy. The Neapolitan pizza bakers are even on the list of intangible UNESCO World Heritage Sites. So if you like sun, beach, and pizza, then this Interrail route is ideal for you. The best pizzas in Naples can be found at L'Antica Pizzeria da Michele or Pizzeria Brandi.

Tip: The Interrail ticket also allows you to use ferries around Italy. These are either free or significantly reduced and are an excellent alternative to the train. From the Italian island of Sicily, the easiest way to get to Livorno is by boat.

Best of Benelux

*Brussels > Bruges > Antwerp >
The Hague > Rotterdam > Amsterdam*

10 Days thereof 7 Travel Days

The Benelux countries can be explored in just 7 days with the Interrail ticket. In Brussels, you will find street art with many exciting stories behind the graffiti and smaller attractions like the market place "Grote Markt" and the landmark "Manneken Pis." The ideal introduction to the city is a free walking tour, visiting all the important sites. From the big city with its tall buildings, the tour continues into picturesque Bruges. Here you will feel like you are in a fairy tale, and you can take lots of beautiful photos.

From Bruges, the journey continues to Antwerp, the capital of diamonds. Here many diamonds were cut and traded in the past. Over time, however, the diamond trade has shifted away from the city. Instead, a few kilos of cocaine pass through the port every day. A full day in Antwerp is enough to explore the city and visit the leading museums. We continue on to The Hague, a Dutch town right on the beach. Depending on how long you want to relax on the beach, one or two days are enough. The city center is not very big but contains many friendly little streets with lovely shops.

From The Hague, you can take the S-Bahn to Rotterdam within 45 minutes, admire the city's architecture, and enjoy the view from the Euromast. For the Rotterdam trip, I would not use the Interrail ticket because a day ticket for the S-Bahn to The Hague costs only a few Euros. You save one day of travel on your passport. The last stop of the journey is Amsterdam, the capital of the Netherlands. Amsterdam is known for its many small waterways called canals and for its beautiful little streets. The city center is very crowded but still worth a visit. On the way, you can either walk or cycle.

Tip: Due to the sometimes required reservations for the TGV trains, it is advisable to plan the travel route and book the train tickets in advance.

Scandinavian Metropolises

Copenhagen > Oslo > Stockholm > Helsinki

15 Days thereof 5-7 Travel Days

The four Scandinavian metropolises can be explored via Interrail in just five days. From Germany, you can quickly reach Copenhagen by train. In addition to the Little Mermaid, the city's landmark, there is also an amusement park in the middle of the city center and the autonomous Christiania quarter, which is well worth visiting. After you have explored Copenhagen, you can continue on the well-developed railway network to Oslo. Here you can explore the Grünerløkka quarter, climb the opera and visit the sculpture park.

If you book seven days instead of five, you can make a detour from Oslo to Bergen with its breathtaking fjords. From Oslo, you can take the train to Stockholm. Here the Skansen Open Air Museum and the photography museum "Fotografiska," as well as the biggest library in the world, are waiting for you. A walk along the harbor is worthwhile, and from here, a ferry to Helsinki regularly starts, which you can use. The overnight trip will fly by, and you can already enjoy your breakfast in Helsinki. If this route is not enough for you, you can even take a ferry, which is not included in the Interrail ticket, to St. Petersburg and use the 72h visa there.

> **Tip:** Due to the short duration of the trip and the sometimes necessary reservations, it is advisable to plan the itinerary in advance and book all reservations.

The beautiful opera house offers a good view of Oslo.

Aurora Explorer

Copenhagen > Stockholm > Kiruna > Rovaniemi > Helsinki

15 Days thereof 5-7 Travel Days

The Scandinavian northern lights attract many travelers to Lapland, which lies far up in the north. You can reach it in only five to seven days of travel. The good thing about traveling by train through the Scandinavian forests is that you can feel Lapland's tranquillity and see how nature changes. From Germany, you can reach the Swedish capital Stockholm via Copenhagen. From there, a night train will take you to Lapland, which is located far to the north. Here you can go for walks through the national park and the vast nature and with a bit of luck, you can even see the northern lights. Via the Finnish city Rovaniemi, you will then continue to the capital Helsinki. From here, you can end your journey with the ferry to Germany.

> **Tip:** Because of the night train you have to book in advance. If you want to see the northern lights, you should travel in winter, as it hardly gets dark in summer. So don't forget your winter jacket and snow boots!

Tour de France

Paris > Toulouse > Marseille > Nice > Lyon

15 Days thereof 7 Travel Days

Most holidaymakers think of Paris when they think of France and not of the many beautiful cities that are still to be explored. My first Interrail tour went through France and showed me the different facets of the country. Paris was only a small stop, as the city is beautiful but very expensive and crowded. Because of this reason, I quickly traveled somewhere else. First in the southwest direction to Toulouse and at the coast further up to Nizza. Via Lyon, it goes back again. Instead of traveling to the south of France, you can visit the Atlantic coast as an alternative. There are also many beaches and beautiful cities to explore.

> **Tip:** From Nizza, you can easily make a day trip to Cannes, the city of the international film festival. But staying overnight there is expensive, it depends on your budget.

Europe Extreme

Germany > Netherlands > Belgium > Luxembourg > France > England > Ireland > Spain > Portugal > Italy > Switzerland > Austria > Slovenia > Croatia > Bosnia-Herzegovina > Montenegro > Serbia > Macedonia > Greece > Turkey > Bulgaria > Romania > Hungary > Slovakia > Czech Republic > Poland > Finland > Sweden > Norway > Denmark

3 Months thereof 30 Travel Days

You have three months and want to see all of Europe? Then the Interrail Pass, with which you can travel for three months without interruption, is worthwhile. During this time, you can travel all the above routes and thus make full use of the Interrail network. There is no exact route for this, as there are countless ways to travel. If you really plan to travel to all European countries in the three months, you have a big task ahead of you and have to expect to spend several days just sitting on the train.

> **Tip:** No matter whether you travel for a week, three months, or a whole year: The amount of luggage always remains the same. Based on my travel experiences, I have, therefore, created an optimized packing list for Interrail.

Popular Night Train Routes

Night trains are becoming more and more popular for train passengers. Most interrailers have used them for a long time. A trip on the night train is an absolute highlight of every journey! Board the train in the evening, enjoy the sunset from your sleeping place, and have breakfast on the train the next morning: a real adventure! But that's not the only thing that makes night trains so popular: longer distances can be covered easily without losing much travel time. There is a higher surcharge for night trains. Still, you save the cost of an overnight stay and have an unforgettable experience!

If you would like to take a night train, you should definitely plan this in advance, as seats are very limited. Most train passengers use the night train right at the beginning or end of their journey. This way, you can quickly reach more distant countries or start your long journey home.

There are several night trains in Europe and countless possibilities to integrate these routes into your own journey. For this reason, I have selected the most popular night train routes for you.

Stockholm - Lapland

Explore Stockholm during the day, fall asleep on the night train in the evening, and have breakfast the next morning in snow-covered Lapland. This route is very popular with travelers to experience the northern lights up close. Possible stops are Kiruna in Sweden or Narvik in Norway.

$\Rightarrow$ sj.se

San Sebastián - Lisbon

The mountainous Basque country of Spain is connected to the coast of Portugal by a night train. In San Sebastián, you can stroll or hike along the seafront promenade; Lisbon offers you a great choice of Portuguese dishes or the imposing fortress, Castelo de São Jorge.

$\Rightarrow$ renfe.com

Milan - Palermo

One day marveling at the cathedral of Milan and the next day lying on the beach in Sicily. This is possible with this overnight train. The train is loaded onto a ferry en route. The Treno Notte takes a total of only 21 hours - including sea views.

$\Rightarrow$ trenitalia.com

Berlin - Vienna

The night train runs from Berlin via Poland and the Czech Republic to Vienna. In the evening you have a view of Brandenburg's forests. The next morning you will have a delicious "Viennese breakfast" before reaching the capital. The Metropol has been running the route from Berlin to Vienna for over 50 years. It has been revived by ÖBB after the old operator MÁV ceased operations.

⇒ nightjet.com

Belgrade - Bar

A trip through the Dinaric mountains is possible with the night train. The mountain railway in Belgrade, Serbia, runs via Bosnia-Herzegovina to Bar, Montenegro. The journey goes over 243 bridges and 254 tunnels, is very varied, and offers breathtaking views.

⇒ srbvoz.rs

Countries & Highlights

Although not all of the countries mentioned above participate in Interrail, they can be explored with separate train or bus tickets. The subdivision is made in the respective regions that do not correspond to the official classification. I have modified them and arranged them according to similarity and travel mentality.

Central Europe

In the center of Europe, some cities could not be more different. There is cultural diversity and tasty local specialties to explore. From an Irish pub in Dublin to a Mona Lisa visit to the Louvre, you can go hiking in the Swiss Alps. The good thing about it is that all countries can be reached very quickly by train and the cultural diversity is only a train ride away. The backpacker community is big here, and if you stay in hostels, you will quickly find a connection.

The best time to travel to Central Europe is from May to September, as it is warm during this period and there are definitely more activities available than in winter. If you don't mind the cold, you can also take advantage of the winter.

Belgium

Belgium is not only known for its cities Bruges and Brussels, but also for its Renaissance architecture. Brussels is the capital of Belgium and the headquarter of the European Union and NATO. Bruges is a fairytale city on the waterfront and invites you to explore the city. Antwerp's port city is a diamond trading center and is famous for its museums and narrow streets.

Germany

Germany is known above all for the major cities like Berlin, Hamburg, and Munich, which could not be more different. While Berlin attracts with its artistic diversity and nightlife, Hamburg is known for its Reeperbahn and the Schanzenviertel, Munich has traditional German beer halls and the Oktoberfest. In addition to the classics, the German metropolises offer international cuisine with a wide variety of tastes.

France

France offers tourists not only good food but also lots of museums and beautiful beaches. The capital city, Paris, is known worldwide for the Eiffel Tower and the Louvre. Trains depart from Paris in all directions of the country, making the capital a good starting point for a trip through France. Besides the capital city, the Côte d'Azur attracts many interrailers.

Great Britain

Although the United Kingdom has not been an Interrail country since 2021, it is worth a visit. London can be reached very quickly from France through the Eurotunnel. The modern city attracts with imposing royal buildings and an original "English Breakfast."

Ireland

Ireland is the green island of Europe and, among other things, also known for its medieval castles and palaces. Dublin is the state capital and the home town of Guinness beer, and the birthplace of writer Oscar Wilde. Interrailers love the pub culture and quiet nature.

Liechtenstein

Liechtenstein's principle is only 25km in size and thus one of the world's smallest countries. The capital Vaduz is the center of the country and offers museums as well as contemporary exhibitions. Outside the city, the Alpine landscape invites you to hike and visit the castles.

Luxembourg

Luxembourg is also one of the world's smallest countries and is somewhat rural with dense forests and nature parks. The same-named capital is known for its medieval old town and is a popular destination for interrailers.

Netherlands

The Netherlands is known for its pretty cities of Amsterdam, Rotterdam, and The Hague. While Rotterdam lures with architecture and The Hague with beaches, Amsterdam offers many small streets, houseboats, and coffee shops. Amsterdam is the first port of call for many backpackers and travelers.

Austria

Austria is located right next to Germany and Switzerland and is the gateway to the Balkan countries. In Austria, you can go hiking through the Alps or explore the capital Vienna with its castles and palaces. If you are interested in the birthplace of Mozart, you should visit Salzburg.

Poland

Poland is very varied and offers something for every interrailer. Hike through the breathtaking landscape, relax on the beach, or explore one of the many museums. Every traveler should definitely try pierogies, which are stuffed dumplings in the most diverse variations. The most popular cities are Warsaw, Krakow, and Gdansk.

Switzerland

Switzerland attracts with its magnificent mountain landscapes, numerous lakes, and beautiful cities. There is no official capital, but there are delicious food and excellent chocolate. If you travel to Switzerland, you can explore the beautiful cities and take many hikes through the mountains. Zurich, Bern, and Geneva are highly recommended for Interailers.

Czech Republic

The Czech Republic is known for its many different types of beer, charming castles and chateaux, and its long historical history. In the medieval Old Town of Prague stands the magnificent Prague Castle from the ninth century. Interrailers appreciate not only the Old Town but also the long party nights here. Walks in the beautiful nature are possible in the Šumava National Park or around the city of Prague. If you are interested in architecture, the town of Český Krumlov is the right place for you.

Scandinavia

Scandinavia is the most northern and, at the same time, the quietest part of Europe. Endless forests, fjords, and cultural diversity in the Scandinavian cities make the region a popular destination for backpackers. Those who like to travel away from the big tourist masses will love Scandinavia. There is an excellent variety of accommodation. It is even possible to camp uncomplicatedly, either on one of the many campsites or wildly in the countryside, according to the "Everyman's Right" which prevails here. It allows you to pitch your tent anywhere and spend a night there. As it can get quite cold and wet in Scandinavia, it is better to camp only in the summertime.

In winter, Scandinavia is dark and cold for a long time, but the summer is pleasantly warm, and it stays light for a long time. For an Interrail journey, summer is ideal in the period from June to September. Nature is very green at this time of year, and you can go hiking or explore fjords by kayak. In the cities, there are many festivals, and there is a relaxed, summery atmosphere. However, if you like winter and want to see the northern lights, you should travel from January to March. During this time, you can also go sledding and go for walks through the endless snowy landscapes.

Denmark

Denmark connects Germany and Sweden with the Öresund Bridge. In the capital Copenhagen, there is the landmark "The Little Mermaid," the Royal Palace, and a little outside of town is the alternative quarter Christiania. The capital has a medieval city center and many small alleys and half-timbered houses.

Finland

Finland is located between Sweden, Norway, and Russia. Its capital is Helsinki. It has several museums and a magnificent designer district. If you prefer nature, you will find it in one of the national parks or in Lapland. For Interrail, we recommend the cities of Helsinki, Turku, and Rovaniemi.

Norway

Norway is known for its fjords, mountains, and glaciers. Not only are nature lovers drawn here: The capital Oslo offers numerous parks and museums and other cultural experiences. From the roof of the opera house, you have a beautiful view over Oslo and the harbor. If you want to relax after your hike, you can take one of the sauna boats. Besides Oslo, Tromsø, Bergen, and Trondheim are worth a visit.

Sweden

Sweden is wildly popular with German backpackers. Besides the diverse nature with its many coniferous forests, there are fascinating big cities like Stockholm, Gothenburg, or Malmö to explore. Here every backpacker will find something suitable. By the way, Stockholm has the biggest library in the world, which you should definitely have a glance at.

Swedish log cabin on the waterfront

Southern Europe

Southern Europe is very popular with backpackers because it is warm, and all countries are located by the sea. The Mediterranean flair and excellent food attract travelers from all over the world to southern Europe. The backpacker scene is big here, and therefore the region is ideal for an Interrail trip.

The ideal travel time for backpacking in Southern Europe is between April and October. During this time, there is a pleasant Mediterranean climate. If you want to avoid tourists' masses, you should not travel between June and August. This is the high season, and it gets boiling. If you still travel at this time, you should pack your swimsuit, as a cooling in the sea is definitely necessary.

Italy

Italy is known for its delicious food, the long Mediterranean coast, and for the masterpieces of Leonardo Da Vinci. The capital Rome offers impressive buildings from the ancient world as well as the Vatican. Other cities worth seeing are Venice with its many small water canals, Milan with its white cathedral, and Pisa with its leaning tower.

Spain

Spain is a popular destination for backpackers because of its warmth and the cultural diversity of the different regions. The capital Madrid and the city of Barcelona are the first points of contact for travelers. Cities like Valencia, Seville, or Granada are also worth a visit. If you would like to visit one of the Balearic Islands, you can reach it easily by ferry with an Interrail reduction on the ticket price.

Portugal

Portugal borders directly on Spain and is extremely popular with surfers. The capital Lisbon is located directly on the Atlantic Ocean and is the fastest way to reach it from Spain. Portuguese cuisine is one of the best in Europe and offers a variety of fish dishes. The country is not only a paradise for surfers, but also for interrailers.

Eastern Europe

The Eastern European countries are often not given much attention, but Eastern Europe has a lot to offer. The less known regions have an adventurous backpacker culture. Interrailers who have been here appreciated Eastern Europe very much. Culturally and historically, there is a lot to discover, and nature invites you to endless hikes and explorations. The big cities offer a wide range of night activities and alternative scenes. A trip here is recommended for every backpacking enthusiast, and with an Interrail pass, this is easy.

The best time to travel to Eastern Europe is from May to August. During this time, it is warm, and many outdoor activities can be undertaken. If you don't mind the cold, you can of course also visit the region in winter. But at this time it is much colder there than in Central Europe.

Estonia

Estonia is one of the easiest countries for backpackers to travel to, as it can be reached directly by ferry from Helsinki. The capital Tallinn has a lovely old town as well as a very nice scene quarter. Estonia has more than 2,000 islands, of which only 18 are inhabited. Particularly worthwhile are Saaremaa and Kihnu.

Latvia

Latvia is ideal for a trip far away from mass tourism. The capital Riga was the European Capital of Culture in 2014 and has a lot to offer. If you like it relatively quiet, the countless national parks are ideal for you or the Latvian seaside resort Jurmala.

Lithuania

In Lithuania, you must see the capital Vilnius. It has countless churches and its own republic called Užupis. If you want to enter this republic, you must take your passport with you. The fun republic was founded on April 1 by creative people and offers you a nice stamp in your passport.

Slovakia

Slovakia is mainly known for its capital Bratislava, but it has a lot more to offer. Hikers are drawn to the High Tatras, the Small Alps of Slovakia, adventurers to the Dobsiná ice cave, and relaxed travelers for Košice culture. During your visit, you should definitely try the country specialty Bryndzové Halušky, cams with Slovak cheese.

Hungary

When you think of Hungary, the first thing that comes to your mind might be Budapest and goulash. The capital was elected as the most popular city by Interrailers. This is partly due to its beautiful architecture, low prices, and the large party scene. But the country has much more to offer. Besides the beautiful capital, there is delicious food everywhere, Lake Balaton and the historic city of Hollókő.

View of Budapest

Balkan Region

The Balkan region often has a bad reputation due to instability. However, the region is underestimated because, for Interrailers, this part of Europe is exciting and full of surprises. While some countries offer a well-developed infrastructure, in others the buses and trains run at will. For example, Croatia has an excellent bus and train network and a large number of ferries to travel from island to island. Whereas in Romania, bus transport is very poor, and train connections are much better.

The ideal travel season for the Balkans is from May to October. In the coastal regions, Mediterranean conditions prevail as in Southern Europe. If you prefer a milder climate, the interior is more suitable for you. In case you want to travel to Macedonia or Albania, you should do so from June to September due to the temperatures.

Albania

Although there is no Interrail in Albania, there is a well-developed bus network, and hitchhiking is possible throughout the country. The capital Tirana is worth a detour and also the karst spring Syri i Kaltër and the castle ruins Rozafa. From Italy, you can get to Albania quickly via Montenegro or by ferry.

Bosnia & Herzegovina

Bosnia & Herzegovina is known for its unspoiled nature and mountainous landscape. As the country is very sparsely populated, it is the ideal destination for friends of nature. It is worth a hike to the Kravica waterfalls or one of the other countless hiking routes. Not only nature lovers get their money's worth here, but also all other travelers. For example, the capital Sarajevo is home to the film festival and has excellent architecture. If you are looking for the perfect photo, you should travel to the Stari Most bridge in Mostar.

Bulgaria

Bulgaria is known for its many beaches and the capital Sofia. It is a very big city, extravagantly built and an ideal stop for train passengers. In addition to the capital, the port city of Varna or Sozopol and the Rila Monastery regularly attract travelers.

Greece

Greece is one of the most uncomplicated countries for backpackers and, with its countless beaches, also one of the most beautiful in the Balkans. It is absolutely diverse and has something to offer for everyone. It is worth exploring the ancient capital of Athens, or you can try island hopping on Crete, Rhodes, or one of the many other islands around the mainland. There is something for every backpacker. An insider tip is the UNESCO monasteries of Metéora near the Pindos Mountains.

Croatia

Croatia is located directly on the Adriatic Sea and is perfect for backpacking. Enjoy coffee in Zagreb's street cafés, relax on Split's beaches, or explore Dubrovnik's old town. By train, Zagreb is the best place to go, and with the ferry, you can travel from Venice directly to the small port city of Pula.

Macedonia

Macedonia is, unfortunately, on the itinerary of very few backpackers, and quite wrongly so. The infrastructure is excellent, the accommodation is cheap, and there is a lot to experience. The first point of contact by train is the capital Skopje. Here an exploration of the old bazaar or a hike to the Millennium Cross awaits you. Adventurers are drawn to Matka Canyon, with more than 5,000 hectares, one of the most popular outdoor travel destinations.

Montenegro

Montenegro could not be more different. While you can ski in the mountains, it is also possible to enjoy the warm temperature in Boka Bay on the same day to enjoy Kotor. Other worthwhile destinations in Montenegro are the Tara Gorge and Biogradska Gora National Park.

Romania

In Romania, many historical cities like Sibiu or Brașov are waiting for you. Here you can start hiking, or you can participate in outdoor activities right after the city tour. You love festivals? Then you should visit the Untold Festival in Cluj-Napoca. The artists are almost the same as at Tomorrowland in Belgium, only the tickets are much cheaper. If the festival doesn't take place, Cluj-Napoca offers you a lot of nature as well as a theme park in an old mine.

Umbrella alley in Bucharest

Serbia

Serbia is an undiscovered country and a real insider tip in Europe. The capital Belgrade is located directly on the Danube and is the best stop for train travelers. Here you will find the Novi Beograd district with its block buildings, the Republic Square with its many sights, and the Kalemegdan Fortress. If you prefer to travel outside the cities, a kayak or mountain bike tour is a good option. In winter, you can even ski in the Kopaonik Mountains.

Slovenia

Slovenia is not overcrowded, although the country can be reached very quickly. This has the great advantage that the country is relatively cheap despite its incredible diversity. The capital Ljubljana is the best place to go by train, and on the way, you can even make a stopover at Lake Bled. A small island on the lake with a pilgrimage church invites you for a walk. Not far away is the Triglav National Park with the country's highest mountain. Flora and fauna of the national park are rich in species, and there are countless mountain paths. Adventurers are attracted by whitewater rafting in addition to hiking.

Turkey

Turkey is a little further away, but an ideal destination in the summertime. In Istanbul, people romp around in the bazaars, and there are many museums to explore. The rest of the country has a lot to offer, too, but this is connected with very long train journeys. Therefore, Istanbul offers you everything your heart desires. Besides culture and bazaars, there is an excellent backpacker scene and lots of great parties.

Backpackers on the Bosporus

5. Accommodation

Finding suitable accommodation has become very easy, thanks to the Internet. But due to the oversupply, it is not so easy to find the right one for you. Therefore, in this chapter, you will find out what types of accommodation are available, how to book them, and what you should pay attention to.

On my first trip, I was unfortunately only in hostels until I got to know the variety of couchsurfing possibilities, affordable hotels, and camping. Not everything will appeal to you, but maybe the one or other overnight accommodation is not as bad as you thought before.

Tip: No matter what you prefer, I have always found the best accommodation through other travelers or travel blogs. Don't rely on reviews on the Internet, but use the knowledge of other travelers.

Tip: In the high season or on public holidays, accommodation can quickly be fully booked. If you already know today where you will be next week, then book promptly. In most cases, you can cancel free of charge.

Hostels

Hostels are the most suitable accommodation for an Interrail tour, as you can quickly meet other travelers and there is usually a good range of activities on offer. Hostels are comparable to youth hostels in Germany but are more aimed at younger backpackers. Hostels are an easy way to meet other travelers and often offer city tours or parties. The rooms range from single rooms to shared rooms for eight people. Hostels are priced between €10 and €40 per night, depending on the country and time of travel and accommodation quality. Useful links:

- ⇒ booking.com
- ⇒ hostelworld.com
- ⇒ hostelbookers.com

You Should Pay Attention to This

Type of Hostel - Some hostels are known for their legendary parties and long nights. If you love to party, these hostels are ideal for you. Everyone else should avoid these hostels as it can get deafening.

Dormitory Size - dormitories for more than ten people, indicate a total rip off hostel. It is cheaper than the others, but the theft rate and the number of partygoers are very high. Basically, the smaller the dormitory, the better you will sleep.

Women's Dormitories - As a woman traveling alone, these dormitories offer a certain amount of security. You can find more information in the chapter Security for Women.

Lockers - To make sure you don't lose anything, your chosen accommodation should have a locker. There is very little theft among backpackers, but this does not mean that it cannot happen.

Location - If the hostel is significantly cheaper than all the others, this may be because it is located far outside the city. Therefore, always pay attention to the distance to the city center.

Cleanliness - Some hostels are really dirty from the kitchen or bathroom up to the bedsheets. You can see the cleanliness in the ratings.

Breakfast - Some hostels offer a free breakfast, but this consists only of toast and cornflakes in many cases. This is not really worth it.

Holiday Flats

Hidden under holiday homes are whole apartments or individual rooms from partly private rentals. Thanks to the new online platforms, everyone can easily offer their place for rent to travelers. This has the advantage for you that you can get central accommodation at a very reasonable price. Depending on the city and location of the apartment, the prices are similar to those of hotels, for a private room or an entire apartment costs between 40€ and 120€ per night. In return, you can often stay there with two people or ideally even with up to four people. Useful links:

- ⇒ airbnb.com
- ⇒ agoda.com

You Should Pay Attention to This

Location - Some accommodations look very good at first sight but are located far outside. If you don't want to spend a long time every day on the bus and train, you should book central accommodation.

Cleanliness - Private accommodation does not always have to be clean. This is often the case in shared flats. You can read about this in the reviews beforehand.

Couchsurfing

At Couchsurfing, you stay with locals who provide you with a place to sleep. They often show you the city, give you insider tips, and thus you get to know the respective city or country differently. Couchsurfing is free, but you should thank your host with a small gift. I have usually invited my hosts to dinner or given them a little something from home. Useful links:

⇒ couchsurfing.com

You Should Pay Attention to This

Big Cities - In big cities you will rarely find accommodation because there is great demand and only a small supply. It's still worth a try, and maybe you will be lucky.

Cleanliness - Read the reviews in advance, as there are some very chaotic couchsurfing hosts. The positive ratings usually indicate a friendly host and only discreetly a dirty or cluttered apartment.

Nudists - There are a few couchsurfers who live as nudists. That means they live naked in their apartment. They often write to travelers and invite them to their apartments under their own conditions. I'd rather not take advantage of such offers!

Men - As a man, you often have a hard time with

couchsurfing, as both hostesses and hosts prefer women. Of course, there is still a chance to find a nice hostess or host.

Women - It is relatively easy for women to get accommodation but also dubious requests from time to time. Therefore, look carefully at who offers you the accommodation or mention your partner several times, so no wrong ideas come up.

BeWelcome

BeWelcome is the best-known alternative to Couchsurfing. Unfortunately, the platform does not have so many users, but it convinces with better functions and more security than Couchsurfing. BeWelcome has the motto "hospitality and cultural exchange."

> ⇒ BeWelcome.org

HelpX

Help Exchange or, in short, HelpX is a platform that supports volunteers in their search for accommodation and connects them with possible hosts. Instead of just looking for accommodation, you will find a host you can help with his daily work. You work 4-5 hours a day on different tasks or projects, and in return, you get free board and lodging.

⇒ HelpX.net

Hotels

Another way to find accommodation is through hotels. These are usually quite expensive compared to other accommodations. If you are traveling in pairs, depending on the country you are traveling to, there can be very cheap offers. In Eastern Europe and the Balkans, for example, there are a lot of affordable hotels. Otherwise, I would instead advise against hotels because you will hardly meet people there as a single traveler.

⇒ booking.com

Camping

Unfortunately, camping is one of the less and less frequently used forms of accommodation. You can stay overnight at campsites or in nature at very reasonable prices. Even if you have to carry your extra luggage, you can still get the most beautiful places to spend the night in the open air. In Scandinavia, the "Everyman's Right" applies, which allows you to pitch your tent anywhere for one night. If you love nature and like camping, this is an excellent way to experience your Interrail tour.

⇒ 1nitetent.com
⇒ tentshome.com

Camping is always an adventure.

6. Budget Planning

In this chapter, we clarify how much money you will need approximately for your Interrail tour. The first thing you should do is to make a rough plan of your route. You will then be able to better estimate your costs and know what equipment you will need. In winter to Sweden? Then you need a winter jacket and a big budget. In summer to Croatia? Then you need a bathing suit and much less money. So plan roughly at which time of the year you want to travel to which country and for how long. More detailed travel planning follows in the following chapters.

Costs for Train Tickets

The first Interrail ticket was available in 1972 and valid for one month. Since then, a lot has changed, and different ticket versions have been added. The costs differ according to the duration, the countries, and whether you have individual travel days or travel in one piece. The longer you travel, the cheaper every trip becomes, but the ticket's total price increases.

Flexible Global Pass

- 4 days - 1 month from 185€ (46€ per day of travel)
- 5 days - 1 month from 212€ (42€ per day of travel)
- 7 days - 1 month from 251€ (36€ per day of travel)
- 10 days - 2 months from 301€ (30€ per day of travel)
- 15 days - 2 months from 370€ (25€ per day of travel)

Continuous Global Pass

- 15 days in a row from 332€ (22€ per day)
- 22 days in a row from 389€ (18€ per day)
- 1 month in a row from 503€ (17€ per day)
- 2 months in a row from 548€ (9€ per day)
- 3 months in a row from 677€ (7,5€ per day)

One Country Pass

The One Country Passes start at 105€ for three days of travel, depending on the country category. But as these are not very interesting, I will refrain from a more detailed version. Sounds cheaper than the Global Pass in the first moment, but you have to pay for the journey yourself, and you can only travel in the chosen country, so it's not really Interrail.

Tip: You can get the reduced price on your Interrail ticket up to the age of 27, and if you book early, you can even get an additional discount of up to 15%.

Reservation Costs

Depending on your travel country, there are additional costs for reservations on your Interrail tour. If you buy these in time, you will save money, as they can become expensive shortly before departure. A reservation is not necessary everywhere. In France, for example, reservations are compulsory for TGV express trains. These range from 6€ to 18€ or, in the worst case, are sold out. The costs vary and range from €3 to €144 per journey, depending on the period and travel country. Don't worry, the 144€ refers to night train rides in a private compartment. If you take a night train, the reservation fee will be much higher, but you will save a night in a hostel. It's hard to estimate what costs you will have to pay. That's why I have conducted a survey with Interrailers about their reservation costs. In short, the survey showed that almost 65% spent less than 60€ on seat reservations.

- Up to 30€   38,9%
- 31€ - 60€   26,4%
- 61€ - 90€   14,5%
- More than 90   20,3%

Train Types

Reservation fees vary depending on the type of train. Here you get a short overview of the most popular train types, including costs. Of course, this is only an example, because the prices can vary.

Regional Trains - For local trains running between smaller towns, reservations are usually unnecessary and not recommended. The trains only travel shorter distances and are usually not very full.

Intercity & Eurocity Trains - Intercity & Eurocity trains run every hour between all major European cities, making it a great way to travel. Reservations are usually unnecessary, but depending on the season, a reservation can make sense, especially in top-rated cities or on weekends.

High-Speed Trains - Reservations are required for high-speed trains, depending on the country. There are only a few exceptions where you do not need to make a reservation in advance. Depending on the number of trains and the season, the train may already be fully booked, and you may have to look for an alternative. According to Interrail, the average price for seat reservations on high-speed trains is €10 for national connections and €15 for international connections.

Night Trains - A trip on a night train is impossible without a reservation, as seats in the couchette or sleeping compartment are limited. The reservation price depends heavily on the desired comfort - first or second class, 3 or 6 berth compartment, and other factors if applicable. Couchette cars are significantly cheaper and differ from sleeping cars with a higher occupancy rate, less privacy, and less comfort. A place in a couchette car costs between €13 and €44 and a place in a sleeping car between €29 and €144. According to Interrail, the average price for night trains is €20 per reservation, which in my opinion is a little too low.

Night trains are the best option for long distances.

Expenditure per Destination

The country costs include the costs for accommodation, food & drinks, activities, and other expenses such as souvenirs. I asked more than 200 travel bloggers about their costs per travel country, resulting in more than 1000 data records. From these data, I have formed the upper and lower mean value. In other words: The cheapest value corresponds to that of an average budget packer, someone who travels rather slowly and takes care of his money, and the most expensive value corresponds to that of an average flashpacker, someone who travels fast and often spends more money. So you can travel even cheaper, but also more expensively.

Costs	Day	Week
Central Europe	36€ - 51€	252€ - 357€
Scandinavia	47€ - 62€	329€ - 434€
Southern Europe	30€ - 40€	210€ - 280€
Eastern Europe	21€ - 29€	147€ - 203€
Balkans	20€ - 28€	140€ - 196€

Cut Expenses

A large part of the money disappears every month without us really noticing it. This is because we have contracts or subscriptions or buy a little something here and there. I always think to myself: 5€ or 10€ per month is not that much money. But 5€ per month is 60€ per year and 10€ is 120€. Calculated over ten years, 10€ per month is more than 1.000€. From this amount, you can afford a nice trip. Here I show you different ways how you can save money in the year before your trip.

Cancel Subscriptions - Do you have current subscriptions for magazines, newspapers, or music streaming? Then think about whether you really need them or if you would rather like to save your money. Instead of Spotify Premium, you can use the free version or use the one to three free months of Deezer or Amazon Music. Depending on the type of subscription, you can save 5€ - 10€ per month. The same applies to magazines or newspapers. You can replace them with exciting blog posts. Depending on your subscription, you can save even more.

Review Contracts - Check your current mobile phone, insurance, DSL, and gym contracts. Sure, there are periods of notice or a deadline to change the deal, but a review always makes sense. With your mobile phone contract, you can usually pay less for the same conditions or get more data volume for the same price. This way, you can either save money or prolong Internet surfing time during your trip. The same applies to DSL and insurance contracts. Here I kept 15€ per contract, which is 180€ per year, and got three gigabytes of additional data volume, which I can use all over Europe.

With your gym membership, you can switch to a free workout in nature or in parks. I haven't been to a gym in seven years and prefer to run in nature and do workouts in parks instead. In other words: 7 years x 12 months x 30€ = 2.520€ = 2 months traveling with Interrail.

Reduce Consumption - A sandwich between meals, a bottle of water here, and a coffee there. Everything usually under two euros, so not so much money after all, right? However, these amounts make up a large amount of possible savings over the year. Making your own coffee in the morning at home, taking a bottle of water with you, and making your own bread saves you a lot of money. I know it's not always easy and doesn't have to be every day, but it saves money. I don't always stick to that myself and buy myself something from time to time.

Gifting Your Equipment - You can have your equipment given to you as a birthday or Christmas present. This will save you a few Euros, and you will receive useful gifts instead of unnecessary items.

Subletting an Apartment - You still have to pay for your own apartment or shared room even though you are traveling, even though you are not using it. Therefore, try to sublet your four walls over the period. There are always people looking for a flat for training or similar purposes or students who have not found a permanent room. I rented my flat once for two weeks and saved half the rent and had someone to water my flowers.

Take Extra Jobs - Small jobs on the side help you to increase your travel budget. These can be simple tasks such as mowing the neighbor's lawn, proofreading texts for a fee, or walking dogs. If you enjoy these things, they are quickly earned Euros. I made a large part of my first trip by mowing the neighbor's lawn. Once a month 15€ and that is a lot of money for 8 years. During my bachelor's degree, I offered weekend courses for children and teenagers on renewable energies. For this, I simply used the knowledge I gained in my lectures and earned 200€ per four-hour workshop. There is always a possibility to make the one or other Euro on the side.

Pay On the Way

Cash - If you are not traveling through Scandinavia, cash will accompany you everywhere. In Europe, this is still indispensable. You should have at least €100 in your wallet so that you can pay cash for a night in your accommodation in case of an emergency if there is no cash dispenser (ATM) nearby. Basically, you can manage with Euros in Europe, unless you travel to Scandinavia, for example. There you pay in Crowns, but there is almost no cash left.

I hardly use cash anymore, but when I travel, I often notice how important it is. For example, I could not pay in a Berlin restaurant, as they only accepted cash. At a flea market in Paris, I didn't have the cash to buy a souvenir, and in Romania, the hotel had to be paid in cash. So you should always have some with you.

EC Card - An EC card is probably something that every traveler can use to withdraw money and pay anywhere in Europe. You can see whether you can use your card by looking at the Maestro sign at the respective cash dispenser (ATM) or card reader. However, the banks have specific regulations regarding the use of the cards, and you should inform yourself about partner banks and their conditions. If you use any ATM, very high fees may apply.

Credit Card - With a credit card, you can pay not only in Europe but also worldwide. It does not matter whether you use a VISA or Mastercard, as both are accepted almost everywhere. When using your credit card, you will usually be charged similar fees to those of the EC card unless you use the right bank. In this case, you will not pay any fees when withdrawing money or paying worldwide. I switched to the DKB credit card over ten years ago and have used it worldwide. This not only saved me many fees but also enabled me to use all cash machines.

Keep the Overview

Your own budget can run out very quickly if you do not have an overview of your costs. Write down your travel budget in advance and estimate your costs approximately. Also, include a 10% buffer in case you have unexpected expenses. You can check how much money you have left or how much more you need to save during the trip. The following apps are suitable for tracking your expenses.

- ⇒ Splid
- ⇒ Tricount
- ⇒ Settle Up

7. Equipment

Planning the Interrail journey is one thing; packing the right things is another. The packing list listed here was created during my travels around the world and has been further optimized by my Interrail journey. This minimalist packing list contains only the most essential things that you really need. There is nothing more annoying than carrying too much luggage and packing and unpacking everything over and over again. If you have forgotten something, you can simply buy it if you need it. With the packing list, it doesn't matter whether you're on the road for a week or three months. The packing list remains the same.

> **Tip:** If you plan on time, you don't have to buy the missing equipment yourself. You can simply wish for it for Christmas, the next birthday, or in between. For example, my backpack was a Christmas present, and the padlocks were for my birthday.

Backpack

A hotly debated question on the Internet is: "Should I use a backpack or suitcase for my trip?" The answer is quite simple: A backpack is the best way for Interrail to travel flexibly. With a suitcase, you are inflexible and immobile because you cannot carry it on your back. I speak from many years of experience in this field, and I am convinced by traveling with backpacks. Practice proves it, you will not see an interrailer with a suitcase on your journey.

There are two differences between travel backpacks. There are large backpacks, also called a backpack, and smaller backpacks also called daypacks. The big one is for your luggage and the routes from place to place and the small one for day trips. A backpack is mandatory, and a daypack optional. I always use a "gym bag" as a daypack. It takes up little space, and I can easily stow it in the backpack.

When buying your backpack, you should choose a reputable brand backpack. They cost between 100€ and 150€, but they last forever. I have been using my backpack for ten years, and it will, for sure, be with me for another ten years. On my travels, I met several backpackers who had cheap 50€ backpacks with which the zippers already broke after one month. The backpack is your most important companion, which you should not skimp on.

> **Tip:** You are not sure which backpack suits you best? A 60-liter capacity is perfectly adequate, and you can try out backpacks in outdoor shops. There, the salesperson will put extra weight in your backpack so that you know how it feels when packed.

A good backpack lasts a lifetime.

Clothing

Opinions differ on the number of clothing items on the packing list, as everyone has a different idea of what is important. For this reason, you should think carefully about what you really need from the listed items and what you can leave at home. To find out how many items of clothing you should take with you, you can use a simple trick:

Put the clothes you want to take with you in the corner of your room and use only these clothes for two weeks. You will soon notice if you are missing something or if you have planned too much. Washing is, of course, allowed, as you can do this during your trip. Everything too much you unpack again, and everything that is missing is added to your Interrail packing list. Here is my suggestion:

- 5 t-shirts - Merino wool is ideal for traveling
- 2 short trousers / skirt / dress
- long trousers - one is quite enough
- thin sweater - for cooler evenings
- thick sweater - in case it gets cold
- 7 socks - in pairs, of course
- 7 underwear - fits the washing rhythm
- sports shoes - for longer distances
- nice shoes - if you ever go out

- swim trunks/bikini - the sea is waiting
- sunglasses - suitable for the beach & city
- rain jacket - in case it should rain

Tip: Most travelers do an Interrail tour in summer, so the list is adapted to this. But if you travel in winter, it is, of course, a good idea to pack a thick jacket, a cap, and a fleece sweater. By the way, the sweater is also very useful in spring and autumn, because it can be cool in the evening and in the morning.

Packing the right amount is the goal.

Toilet Bag

Almost everything that you need at home, you should take with you on your journey. Preferably smaller, leak-proof, and lighter. In my list, I, therefore, link to good alternatives for your Interrail tour. Of course, you can simply buy your bathroom utensils at one of the big drugstore chains, but the travel sizes are much more expensive and not environmentally friendly. By the way, you can leave a travel hair dryer at home, as all accommodations offer a hairdryer for rent.

- toothbrush & -pasta
- solid travel soap
- microfibre travel towel
- shaver & Shaving Foam
- sun cream
- first aid kit in travel size
- personal medicines
- other hygiene articles

Tip: You can store everything compactly in a travel toilet bag and hang it up in the bathroom in your accommodation. You can also fold it up quickly, and it has extra leak protection for liquids.

Documents

You should keep all your essential documents in one place. The best way to do this is with an organizer or a compartment in your backpack. On all trips, whether Interrail or not, the most important items are always your passport and cash/credit card. Everything else can be replaced. A stolen backpack can be bought later, but missing money causes much bigger problems, and it is harder to get. The same applies to your ID/passport, although it is not quite as bad in Europe as in other countries. So always take extra care of these two things!

- interrail pass
- identity card or passport
- cash - is always good
- travel credit card
- debit card
- traveljournal - diary & travel planner
- european insurance card
- vaccination card & allergy passport
- interrail map
- travel guide
- diving license

Camping

If you are traveling with a tent during your Interrail adventure, your packing list will contain a little more equipment. The most essential items are a tent, a sleeping bag, and a sleeping mat. Of course, you can pack much more, but you should pay attention to the weight.

- sleeping bag
- tent
- isomat

Miscellaneous

Miscellaneous includes all electronic devices as well as objects that I could not classify otherwise. As in the other categories, only the basics are listed here, and you can add your personal items individually.

- camera - memory card & spare batteries
- charging cable - for Smartphone & Camera
- ebook reader & audio book app
- headphones - for music & audiobooks
- earplugs - there are snoring interrailers
- sleeping mask - just in case
- water bottle - saves a lot of money
- lock - for the locker in the accommodation

Travel Guide

A travel guide is worthwhile because you get a good overview of the country. In addition to current information about lodging, there are events and much more. However, a travel guide is not mandatory, but rather an easy way to get information quickly and compactly. In my opinion, travel blogs are quite sufficient to get information about the respective countries or cities. A travel guide's advantage is that the information is updated every two years, and you always get the full range of information. Most travel blogs, mine included, report more about activities that the blogger likes and that you might not like. I love photography and always mention a photo museum in my posts, but sometimes I leave out the well-known sightseeing places. If you don't want to use a travel guide, you have to find a travel blogger that suits you.

Lonely Planet Europe

The Lonely Planet Europe offers you all the information you need about all the countries in Europe. Here you can find everything from the metropolis to small towns. You will get tips for sightseeing, accommodation, and restaurants. However, the Lonely Planet is huge and heavy, as really all countries are described. If you travel to a specific region, a travel guide only makes more sense for this region.

Lonely Planet, the Best Things in Life are for Free

Instead of a paid travel guide, you can also use the free travel guide from Lonely Planet. This contains the best and, at the same time, free highlights from all over the world. For Europe, there are some excellent tips and maps of the major cities. The travel guide is in English, but it is very easy to understand, and did I mention it? Free of charge!

⇒ Backpacker-Dude.com/BOOK/FreeTravelGuide

Interrail Card Marco Polo Card

The Marco Polo publishing house has created a waterproof Interrail map on which you will find all routes listed by country. In addition to the route network, you will also find the necessary information about the country you are traveling to. You know in advance which travel adapter you will need and what you should definitely check out in each state.

Interrail Card Free of Charge

Instead of a purchased map, you can also use the free Interrail map. This offers you all train routes, approximate travel times, and the whole of Europe at a glance. If you use the map with the information in this book, you don't have to spend extra money. You can find the plan online in advance and print it out together with your ticket by post.

⇒ Backpacker-Dude.com/BOOK/FreeMap

Printed or Digital

Is a travel guide or a map in paper form still worthwhile if available in digital format at a lower price? Yes and no, a printed travel guide invites you to leaf through it and discover places by chance. A printed map is much better, especially for route planning. Besides, the printed version is always available and works without electricity. A disadvantage is the weight of thicker travel guides, and this takes up space in the luggage. If you choose a map, I recommend taking a printed version with you. If you want to use a travel guide, you have to consider whether you take a printed or digital version with you.

Unnecessary

The official Interrail packing list is unfortunately not recommended, as it contains some unnecessary things. For example, it is recommended to take an alarm clock with you, which everyone has already integrated into their smartphone. A bottle opener and swimming goggles are also recommended. Seriously!? If you are a backpacker and can't open a bottle without a bottle opener in an emergency, you should rather stay home and go swimming. With swimming goggles, of course! Just fun, but there is really a lot of useless stuff you can leave at home. Here are some examples:

- alarm clock
- backpack net lock
- hammock
- travel washbag
- astronaut Food
- money belt

How Much to Pack?

Packing the right amount of luggage is not easy, but this packing list will give you a good guideline for your Interrail tour. It doesn't matter whether you are traveling for a few days or even four weeks. Complete the packing list as you wish, or just leave some items out. You will undoubtedly notice within the first days of your journey that you have forgotten something. However, this is not a problem, as you can borrow or buy anything you need. This is better than finding out at the end of the trip that you have carried too many unnecessary items and, therefore, could not travel flexibly. Therefore it is better to pack too little than too much.

> **Tip:** A perfect backpacker trick is to put an empty shoebox into the backpack while packing. Naturally, this is removed again before the journey starts, but you have some spare space in your backpack (for example, for souvenirs).

8. Safety

Europe is the safest continent in the world. Medical care is excellent. You can also communicate everywhere in English. The worst thing that can happen to you is that you make a stopover in a place that bores you to death. However, to prepare for all eventualities, you will find out how to protect yourself and what you can do in each case.

Securing Documents

The best way to secure a copy of your ID, passport, or vaccination card is to use a cloud. You can use the free storage space of one of the renowned cloud providers. A better alternative is to use the online safety of your online banking. Almost all online banks offer you some online storage to back up your most important data. I secure my passport, vaccination card, and other documents, such as my driving license there. If you lose one of your papers, you will always get a digital copy.

- ⇒ dropbox.com
- ⇒ drive.Google.com
- ⇒ box.com

Pickpocketing

Theft is everywhere, and you can hardly resist it, whether at home or on the road. But there are useful tips on how you can protect yourself. You can also find out what to do if you lose your credit card or smartphone.

- valuables & wallet
  wear close to the body
- take little cash with you and
  do not show this openly
- one debit or credit card in your wallet
  and one in your luggage
- caution with mixtures and
  supposed incitements

Identity Card Lost

Losing your identity card or passport in Europe is relatively harmless compared to other countries. The only important thing is that you report it as stolen or lost. Otherwise, it can be used by criminals. Unfortunately, there are always scams with false identity documents. However, if your documents are reported to the police, the likelihood of fraudsters using them is much lower.

You can apply for a new identity card or passport during your trip and pick it up at one of the consulates.

Depending on how long your journey still lasts, this may not be worthwhile. If necessary, you can also check in with a copy of your passport at your accommodation. If you have to identify yourself without any documents, in the worst case, this may involve a visit to a police station where your personal details will be clarified. You can obtain a new identity card or passport from the embassy or consulate in each country.

Credit Card Lost

Do not panic. You can block your card at any time and thus render it unusable. However, you should be sure that your card has really been lost and is not in your backpack somewhere. If your card is definitely lost or stolen, you must block it immediately. Most banking apps have a temporary and a permanent blocking function. If you are not using a banking app or the process does not exist, you can call the general blocking number 116 116.

If your card is blocked, you should make a report to the local police. You will not get your card back, but you are covered for consequential damages. You will then have official confirmation of the loss and, in the case of unknown debits, proof of the loss. If you do not report the loss, you could end up with the resulting costs.

Once your card is blocked and you have created an ad, you can apply for a new card at your bank. You can have it sent to one of the following accommodation facilities. However, you should check this with the accommodation and your bank in advance. To bridge the time without a card, you can borrow cash from other travelers and reimburse them directly by bank transfer.

Tip: Card and PIN should not be kept together. If your card and PIN are stolen, your bank does not have to replace the money. If you can't remember your PIN, it's better to save a telephone number that contains the PIN. This is transparent but more secure than a piece of paper with the PIN next to the card. Max Sampler 0178 / 123 **4513**

Smartphone Lost

Call your mobile operator immediately and have your SIM card blocked. Use other travelers' smartphones or ask at your accommodation if you can make a quick call. You can find the phone numbers of the respective provider on the Internet, as there currently no general blocking number. If you don't block your SIM card in time, you may be charged expensive fees for calls abroad or dubious phone numbers. This also applies to prepaid cards!

When your SIM card is blocked, your mobile operator will send you a new one. This usually takes longer than a week and is therefore very impractical. It's better to buy a cheap mobile phone and prepaid card locally and use it until the end of your trip. You can use the SIM card throughout Europe without any additional charges due to European laws. You can find out more about using SIM cards in the chapter Phone & Internet.

Tip: If you use an iPhone, you can use iCloud to delete all your phone data. Other manufacturers have a similar function.

Security for Women

Although I am a man, I have spoken a lot with women about security during my travels. So here is a summary of my experiences of women traveling alone. Europe is basically a very safe travel area for women, and the same safety rules apply as in your home country.

Say No - learn to say no and communicate it clearly. There are always very pushy men. If you don't say no to them clearly and distinctly, you will, unfortunately, not get rid of this kind of person. Set clear boundaries and use the word "no" because a hesitant "rather not" or "reluctantly" is often perceived by such people as an indirect "yes." You MUST practice this. Otherwise, you can get into very unpleasant situations.

Clothing - Wear clothing that is not too tight. Sure, it doesn't have to be that you are directly hit on by some men because of your tight clothes. However, you are more likely to get chatted up if you walk around belly-free or in a mini dress. This is especially true if you are traveling alone.

Lying - Helps you in some situations. Whether you have a boyfriend or not doesn't matter. If you are not sure about a man's intentions, tell him about your boyfriend and that he is coming or waiting for you. This already scares many people off, and you have your peace. I have used this trick even with pushy women, and it works wonderfully.

Women's Dormitories - Almost all hostels offer women's dormitories, giving you peace of mind. Men do not have access here, and they are usually closer to the reception. I have not heard many sensitive stories about dormitories over the years, but just to be on the safe side.

Ask for Help - If you are in a delicate situation, talk to other people. Most people don't help because they think that there are enough others, and in the end, nobody helps. If you speak to someone directly, you will get help.

Darkness - Do not stay out alone at night. If you have to go shopping late, just ask someone to accompany you. If you want to go on a pub crawl or party, make sure you know who will be accompanying you on the way back. There is always someone who wants to go back at the same time.

Outdoor Safety

Bears & Wolves - Yes, there are bears and wolves in Europe, but not very many and only in remote places. Mainly there are bears in Scandinavia and in the Balkan region. Wolves can be found everywhere in Europe. If you are hiking in mountainous areas or deep forests, there is a very low probability that you will see a wolf or bear. Then you should try to keep as much distance as possible. Camping can be different because hungry bears smell your food and are attracted by it. Basically, there is no danger of bears or wolves. There are often warning signs in the respective regions telling you how to behave in a sighting case.

Landmines - Yes, there are many landmines in Europe, more precisely in Croatia and the Balkan region. Bosnia-Herzegovina is the worst affected, but there is no danger for you. The mined areas are outside the travel regions and are additionally signposted.

9. Health

It can quickly happen that you have an accident during your journey. When crossing the road, you do not pay attention, or you slip while hiking. Luckily, Europe has an excellent health system that protects you. Nevertheless, you should always act with foresight. For example, road traffic is not still so civilized, and people drive in a very unreasonable way. Then you should act with greater caution. The same applies to outdoor activities. For example, if you have never been hiking before, an accessible route makes more sense than an extreme one for mountain professionals. I chose the second example because I saw a list of dead backpackers before a hiking trail, all of whom died on this route. Above it was the warning: This route is not for beginners and is always overrated. Despite the sign, the last advertisement was just one year old.

Emergency Telephone Numbers

In an accident or other emergency, it is vital to remain calm and call 112. This number connects you to the police, ambulance, or fire brigade throughout Europe. Answer the W questions at the emergency call center: Who is calling? What has happened? Where did it happen? How many people are affected? Wait for further questions!

European Health Card

The European Health Insurance Card (EHIC) ensures you across borders, and you can use it to receive medical services in the EU and some other European countries. If you have an accident or acute complaints, you are entitled to medical services. You simply go to the doctor and present the card as usual and get treatment. Your health insurance company will then cover the costs for you. If you have to pay cash in advance, you can submit it to your health insurance company afterward.

The health card is usually located on the back of your insurance card. So you do not need to apply for it separately. I didn't know that myself and had to pay 160€ for the doctor in Sweden. My health insurance company reimbursed me the costs afterward, but I had to advance everything. If I had simply gone to the doctor without acute complaints, I would not have got the money back. This also applies, for example, to chronic illnesses or illnesses with special medical supervision. You have to clarify this with your health insurance company in advance.

The EHIC applies here:

- Belgium
- Bulgaria
- Denmark
- Estonia
- Finland
- France
- Greece
- Greenland
- Great Britain
- Ireland
- Iceland
- Italy
- Croatia
- Latvia
- Liechtenstein
- Lithuania
- Luxembourg
- Malta
- Montenegro
- Netherlands
- Macedonia
- Norway
- Austria
- Poland
- Portugal
- Romania
- Sweden
- Switzerland
- Serbia
- Spain
- Slovakia
- Slovenia
- Czech Republic
- Hungary
- Cyprus

International Health Insurance

International health insurance is usually not necessary for an Interrail tour. Unless you travel to Turkey or other countries that are not covered by the EHIC health card. The countries listed here refer to the pan-European area and are listed for completeness.

- Andorra
- Antilles
- British Channel Islands
- Faeroe Islands
- Isle of Man
- Kosovo
- Monaco
- San Marino
- Svalbard
- Turkey

For short trips to these countries of less than 56 days, a simple travel health insurance is sufficient, probably the case for all Interrail journeys. However, if you wish to travel longer, long-term insurance is necessary. With this, you can travel longer than 56 days and are insured worldwide. I have been insured with Hanse Merkur for years and never had any problems with it. The refunds are fast, and the service is excellent.

Vaccinations & Precaution

"Vaccinations are among the most important and effective preventive measures available in medicine to protect against infectious disease. Modern vaccines are well tolerated, and adverse drug reactions are rarely observed. Protective vaccinations not only have an effect on the vaccinated persons (personal protection) but can also indirectly protect non-vaccinated persons from a disease, as they stop or reduce the further spread of an infectious disease (community protection)." This is what the Federal Ministry of Health says, and therefore it makes sense to see your doctor before you travel. He can check and refresh your vaccinations. Basically, you do not need any extra vaccinations for your trip, but they should be up to date. The Federal Ministry of Health recommends:

- Poliomyelitis
- Measles vaccination
- Diphtheria (refresh every 10 years)
- Tetanus (refresh every 10 years)
- Pertussis (refresh every 10 years)

Optional Vaccinations

Hepatitis A - Can be transmitted anywhere through contaminated drinking water, contaminated food, or as a smear infection. Hepatitis A occurs in the temperate latitudes, including Europe. The vaccination is covered by most health insurance companies.

Hepatitis B - Hepatitis B, the most common viral infection, can be transmitted through all body fluids. If you belong to a risk group or are traveling outside Europe, vaccination may make sense. Some health insurance companies require you to pay for the immunization yourself.

Rabies - The risk of rabies is higher in the Balkan region than in Central Europe. If you travel to this region, vaccination may be useful. A complete rabies vaccination, consisting of three vaccinations, costs around 200€ and lasts for 5 years.

You can decide together with your doctor which of these vaccinations make sense.

10. Practical Tips

There are many good but also some nonsensical tips for traveling. You will soon notice which tips are useful for you and which are not. I have, therefore, limited myself here to my most important information. If you meet other travelers in their accommodation, you can ask them for local tips: maybe some museums have free admission on certain days.

Interrail Groups - Join all the relevant Interrail groups on Facebook to keep you up to date. There you can ask for tips for the respective city, search for travel partners, or exchange information about train connections with other Interrail users.

- Interrail Travelers Official
- Interrail Travelers
- #DiscoverEU Official

Language Barriers - Admittedly, almost all younger Europeans speak English. If you think your English is not very good, it doesn't matter. You do not have to pass an exam on your journey. Besides, you will get used to speaking English quickly. I spoke very poor English on my first backpacking adventure, and meanwhile, my English is fluent without ever attending an English class again.

Besides English, it always helps to know a few words or sentences in the local language. This creates a certain kind of closeness with strangers and is very helpful. You can look up the most important words on the Internet or download an app on your mobile phone.

- duolingo.com
- babbel.com

Telephone & Internet - The European law on data roaming, which came into force in June 2017, will allow you to keep your home tariff. You can, therefore, continue to use your free minutes and data volume. It does not matter which European country you are in, only how long you stay. Depending on the provider, at least two months are possible without any problems, and only after that, the more extended stay abroad must be justified.

Nearly all accommodations and restaurants also offer Wi-Fi hotspots, which allow you to surf for 30 minutes or more. There are also a lot of free hotspots in all major cities. You can find them quickly by using one of the listed apps.

- ⇒ wifimap.io
- ⇒ wefi.com/wefi-app

I know from myself that I sit at my smartphone too often and somehow ruin my travel time. To make sure that you will remember your trip long and positively, leave your smartphone out often. If you get lost, don't look directly, just ask other people or explore the newly discovered area.

Offline Maps - Connected to the Internet, you have access to all maps. But you should also be prepared for dead spots or other bad connections. The app "MapsMe" is the most popular because you can download the respective country map and always have it with you when you're offline.

⇒ mapsme.com
⇒ maps.google.com
⇒ wego.here.com

Tips for Train Travel

Use the Interrail App - This includes all the train connections you can use and even offline. In the Interrail app, you can also filter the trains according to the reservation requirement and travel more cheaply. The only disadvantage of the app is that you will not be shown any delays or cancellations. However, you can do this online with the respective railway company.

Comfortable Train Travel - Traveling by train every few days can be exhausting. Of course, it's fun to watch the landscape rushing by, but at some point, it gets boring, or sitting is annoying. To prevent this from happening to you, you will find all the essential information you need for a relaxed train journey in this chapter.

- **Punctuality** - Being at the station on time saves you not only stress but also possible rescheduling of your route. Once you have chosen a suitable route and perhaps even made a reservation, nothing is more annoying than missing the appropriate train.
- **Book & Travel Guide -** A good book and a useful travel guide should not be missing on your train trips. You can shorten your travel time and get new input.

- **Audiobook & Podcasts** - A good audiobook or podcast is like a good book. You can dive into other worlds with it or even inform yourself about the upcoming travel destination because there are many travel accessory books or podcasts about your travel destinations.
- **Scenic Routes** - If you choose one of the many scenic routes before your departure, you will have a relaxed ride, as the view is even more beautiful. A beautiful train route is an absolute experience for every Interrail tour.
- **Plan Your Itinerary** - You certainly already have your next destination in mind and can plan your route there on the train. The free Interrail map or the Interrail app will help you do this.
- **Conversations** - Whether you travel alone or with a travel partner, a good conversation is quickly started. Simply greet your seatmate when you sit down and find out whether he or she feels like talking.
- **Sort Photos** - You can use the train ride to sort your previous images. Then you don't have to do all this when you return.
- **Eating in the Dining Car** - The food here is better than I always thought. Especially in Eastern Europe and in the Balkans, the prices are very

reasonable, and there is a large selection of delicious food.
- **Writing a Travel Diary** - A diary is the best way to record places and memories that you might have forgotten.
- **Comfortable Clothing** - Especially on very long journeys, comfortable clothing is almost a must, as you cannot change well on the train itself.
- **Bring a Pillow** - If you want to sleep on the train, a pillow can be beneficial. To save space, you can take an inflatable pillow or just a soft sweater.
- **Using Night Trains** - My absolute favorite for very long distances are night trains. There is a small extra charge, but the journey goes by in no time.

The 19 o'Clock Trick - Unfortunately, this trick no longer works. With this one, it was possible to take an Interrail train from 19 o'clock on and use only one day of travel, namely the following day, as a travel day. Especially with night trains, this was an optimal possibility to save one day of travel. The one or other backpacker will still tell you that this trick works. But this is not true anymore!

According to the new regulations, you need a full travel day for a night train trip. If the night train leaves at 10 pm on April 14 and arrives at 8 am on April 15, this is a day of travel in your Interrail Pass. If, for example, you would like to travel somewhere else on April 15, an extra day of travel is required.

Add Travel Days - If you find that your Interrail contingent is not sufficient, you can simply add a few travel days. In return, you can travel some routes with a different ticket. Cheap alternatives are, for example, the FlixBus or a carpool. This works best for short connections because, with the Interrail Pass, you should instead use the more expensive, long connections. You may also have the opportunity to hitchhike part of your route. This tip works very well in southern and eastern Europe.

Tips for Thrifty

Win an Interrail Ticket - Are you still 17 or just turned 18? Then you have the chance to win an Interrail pass and travel through Europe free of charge for 30 days. You can even take part as a group of up to five people. All you have to do is indicate this when you register. You have to pay for food and accommodation yourself, but there is no extra cost for the ticket. The following requirements are necessary for the raffle:

- You are 18 years old or about to be.
- You are an EU citizen of the 28 countries
- You meet the application deadline
- You become DiscoverEU Ambassador
- You travel up to 30 days through Europe

How you have to proceed precisely with the registration, you will find out in my detailed article. When the next raffle takes place is announced on the website of DiscoverEU.

⇒ Backpacker-Dude.com/BOOK/DiscoverEU

Travel Without Reservation - Only 6% of all interrailers travel without having made a single reservation. The advantage is that there are no extra costs and you travel economically. The disadvantage is that you can do without high-speed trains and switch to slower trains. With good planning and a suitable destination, it is possible to travel without a reservation.

Free Walking Tours - A good option for a free city tour is Free Walking Tours. You will be shown the city with all its interesting and historical places and in the end, you "pay" the tour guide with a tip. The Free Walking Tours are fascinating, informative, and you will learn some fun facts about the city.

If you don't like a tour, that's not a problem, because you can just leave it and you don't owe anything to anyone. If you liked it, three to five euros is a good tip for the tour guide. I have already joined these tours in many European cities, and I was always amazed!

At the end of the tour, the tour guides will always give you tips for restaurants or places you might be interested in. You can find the Free Walking Tours by searching on Google for "Free Walking Tour + city name." In Western Europe, "Sandemans New Europe" is the leading provider, and in Eastern Europe, "Free Walkative."

⇒ neweuropetours.eu
⇒ freewalkingtour.com
⇒ freetoursbyfoot.com

Low-Cost Travel Countries - The 31 participating Interrail countries differ significantly in terms of travel costs. While you can get accommodation for a few Euros in the Balkans, you have to pay up to five times as much per night in Scandinavia. In other words, you can travel with the same amount of money, in one country for a week and in another for a whole month. You save the most money in Eastern Europe and the Balkan region. In these countries, you don't have to book a reservation, and you save a few Euros again.

Cheap Accommodation - If you have chosen an expensive destination, there is still the possibility of saving money on accommodation. Either you book cheap hostels, which are rather on the city's outskirts, or you try couchsurfing. Hostels on the city's outskirts are usually much less expensive, but you have to be prepared for a longer walking distance to go to the city center. Couchsurfing is free of charge, and you get to know the respective place through a local who has been living there for a longer time. No matter what you choose, the main thing is that you feel comfortable. I regularly publish the current actions to save money offered by the booking platforms. If you are redirected to the regular website, there is no action at the moment.

Free Museum Visits - Some museums offer free admission on certain days of the month. You can find out which museums and days these are at your accommodation or from the tour guides of Free Walking Tours. For example, on the 1st Sunday of the month, all museum admissions are free in France. If you are 25 or younger, you can go to French museums every day for free. All you have to do is show your identity card, and you will receive a free ticket.

Take a Water Bottle With You - A refillable bottle saves you a lot of money because you don't have to buy expensive water. Tap water is drinkable everywhere, thanks to European laws. Therefore, it is better to refill it for free and save money instead of looking for a supermarket and paying for every water drop.

Free Travel Credit Card - withdrawing money abroad can quickly become expensive. You can use your EC card in most European countries, but you will have to pay high fees in many cases. These charges can be made when you withdraw money or when you pay with your card. These fees are often ignored and can add up to a large amount at the end of your trip.

Take Advantage of Interrail Benefits - One of the biggest savings tips for your journey is the additional benefits of the Interrail Pass. With it, you can use bus and ferry connections at reduced rates, get discounts at museums, and even in selected accommodation. In combination with the ISIC card mentioned above, you can save money in many places. Just don't use these offer discounts blindly, because they might tempt you to spend more money. A hostel night for 15€ is still cheaper than a hostel night for 20€ with a 20% discount!

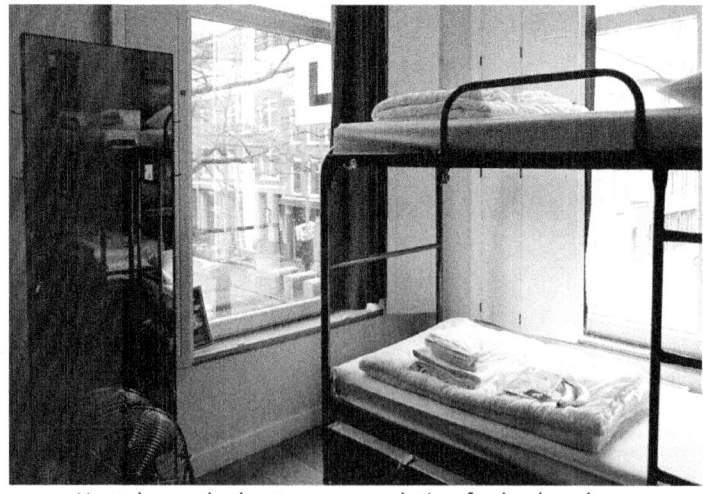

Hostels are the best accommodation for backpackers.

Cooking Tips

When traveling, cooking comes, unfortunately, always a bit short, although it is the best way to get to know other travelers and get by with little money. During my travels, I made many friends through cooking and got to know travel partners for the next stage. Therefore, here is a listing of recipes that you can make quickly and easily on the way and tips for surviving in the hostel kitchen.

Use Weekly Markets - restaurants can be costly, depending on the country. If so, you should instead cook for yourself and use backpacker recipes. Almost all towns have small weekly markets where you can buy fruit, vegetables, and other ingredients at reasonable prices. When the weekly markets close, the costs are usually reduced again, making it worthwhile to buy late.

Pancake Recipe - My absolute highlight recipe is made very quickly with few ingredients and is popular with all travelers. The Backpacker Pancakes require only three ingredients, which are simply mixed together. Then put them into a lightly oiled pan and enjoy it with the side dish of your choice.

- 1x cup of flour
- 1x cup of milk

- 1x egg or banana

For breakfast, maple syrup, jam, or Nutella is suitable. If you have pancakes left over, you can take them with you as a snack on the road or in the evening with cheese, hummus, or avocado cream. You can replace the milk with a vegetable alternative or mineral water and the egg with a banana if you are vegan. If you prefer the pancakes fluffy, just add some baking powder.

One-Pot-Pasta Recipe - This recipe was definitely developed by backpackers because it is cooked super quickly in only one pot. You simply cut all the ingredients into small pieces, cook them together with the pasta in the pot, and serve them afterward. If there is some water missing, you can add it, and as soon as the noodles are al dente, your meal is ready.

- 250g spaghetti
- 1 onion
- 1 garlic clove
- 100g mushrooms
- some cocktail tomatoes
- 1 can of strained tomatoes
- salt, pepper, and oregano
- 0,5-liter water
- 1 stock cube

This recipe contains many ingredients, but all are optional, and you can omit some or add others. How about zucchini or eggplant, for example? Or add a regional spice? There are no limits to what you can cook.

Curry Recipe - This recipe is a very simple and versatile curry to cook on the go. Other ingredients can be used as you like, depending on what you have at hand.

- 2 carrots
- 1 can of chickpeas
- 1 can of coconut milk
- 250g chicken breast, beef, or tofu
- red curry paste
- salt & pepper
- jasmine rice

Optional

- green beans
- red pepper
- bean sprouts
- one onion
- chilli pepper

Cut the meat or tofu into small pieces and fry it in the pan. Then add the chickpeas and the chopped vegetables and deglaze with coconut milk. Finally, cook with the red curry paste and a little salt and pepper. The curry is served with rice.

Hostel Kitchens - When traveling, you have to be creative in cooking and know the trade tricks for hostel kitchens. Otherwise, it can quickly happen that you don't get to cook or even lose your tasty food.

- **Label** - Label all your food before you put it on any shelf or in the refrigerator. Hostel kitchens are cleaned regularly, and unlabelled food is often thrown away. The label should show your name, room number, and date of departure. If you leave and forget your food, it will be easier to sort it out. It is best to pack all your groceries in a large bag so that you do not have to label everything individually.
- **Refrigerator** - Only what needs to be cooled belongs in the fridge. Otherwise, it becomes too full, and others cannot put anything else in it. In the worst case, you are the unlucky person who has to store fresh milk and cheese outside the fridge. If there is any cooked food left, you can put it on a plate and put it in the refrigerator with a cling film. Pots and pans in the fridge are sorted out directly.

- **Simple Cooking** - The simpler the recipes are, the fewer ingredients you need, and the less you have to carry around. So use simple recipes and only buy what you will use within the next two days.
- **Clean Kitchen** - Leaving the kitchen clean may sound a bit strange, but as soon as the first backpacker leaves the kitchen untidy, some people join to do the same. Even if the kitchen is cleaned regularly, you should always try to leave it in a clean condition yourself.

Hostel kitchens quickly become untidy.

Tips for Adventurers

Discover Smaller Cities - Of course, there is a reason why certain cities are so popular with travelers. Paris offers the Eiffel Tower, Venice the gondola canals, and Rome the Colosseum. These are all exciting cities and definitely worth a visit. However, even smaller places offer you many possibilities and experiences away from the tourist masses. A stopover in a Portuguese fishing village, a hike in Albania, or a festival in Romania, most travelers have not yet experienced. Besides, the accommodation there is usually cheaper, and couchsurfing is much more comfortable. In small villages, there are fewer travelers and often a better choice of hosts.

Explore Local Specialties - During your Interrail tour, you can save money by eating locally and cooking for yourself from time to time. It has two advantages to eat local food: you get to know the country's food culture and support local restaurants. Each destination has its own recipes and a variety of tastes. In Poland, for example, you should try pierogies, in Sweden köttbullar, and in Spain a paella.

Travel Diary & Blog

During your Interrail adventure, you will experience quite a lot. Some things stay in your head for a lifetime; others you unfortunately forget. To not let this happen to you, a travel diary or blog is the perfect way to record personal experiences. I write down my experiences, look at them regularly, and am always happy about them.

A travel diary offers you the opportunity to write down your experiences and complement them with personal thoughts and pictures. Also, you can paste in tickets, or other travelers can immortalize themselves in it. A simple notebook, daily planner, or travel diary is suitable for this purpose.

A blog is a great way to record your journey for yourself and others. It's a place to capture less personal thoughts, but you can share your stories with family and friends. If you write in an informative way, your contributions might even be listed on Google, and you can help other interrailers with your experiences.

11. Conclusion

You have now learned everything you need to know about train travel in Europe and what you need for your journey. With these preparations, I hope I have taken away your fears and uncertainties. As you have read the book to the end, I hope that you will decide to take an adventure by train through Europe and get to know this continent differently. So what are you waiting for? Let's go, your adventure awaits!

I wish you a breathtaking Interrail tour with many big and small adventures that you will remember for the rest of your life. Or as Mark Twain said:

"Twenty years from now, you will be more disappointed by the things you didn't do than by the ones you did do. So throw off the bowlines, sail away from the safe harbor. Catch the trade winds in your sails. Explore. Dream. Discover."

Questions & Remarks

If you liked my book, please leave an honest review on Amazon. If you have a question or comments that I could not answer in the book, please send me an email to Question@Backpacker-Dude.com. I will answer you as soon as possible when I am not traveling myself.

Acknowledgment

At this point, I would like to thank all the people who helped me to write this book. It is only through you that it has become possible to realize this idea. Special thanks to Ines Muñoz Zúñiga, who proofreads the book, and Nik Neves, who did the cover design. Furthermore, I would like to thank Laura, Hannah, Manuel, Amadeus, and Heike for their helpful feedback and all the interrailers who gave me the idea. Thanks a lot!

Picture Credits

Amelie's field report © Madeleine Ragsdale

Rubens' field report © Clem Onojeghuo

Nina's field report © Simon Maage

Lena's field report © Seth Doyle

Buying Tickets © Claudio Schwarz

Get to Know People © Helena Lopes

Accommodation Camping © Scott Goodwill

Route example Scandinavia © Arvid Malde

Country description Sweden © Inès d'Anselme

Country description Romania © Haseeb Jamil

Country description Hungary © Bence Balla-Schottner

Country description Turkey © Meriç Dağlı

Night train © Jonathan Barreto

Backpack Packing List © Josiah Weiss

Clothing Packing © Sarah Brown

Hostel Room © Marcus Loke

Links

It is actually very unusual to put links in a book, but the ongoing digitalization and periodic updates make it necessary. This is why I partly use the Backpacker-Dude.com/BOOK/Links, because I can change them at any time through my travel blog. So you have simpler, mostly shorter links and always linked to the current website.

Printed in Great Britain
by Amazon